D1637193

FREEDOM IN OUR LIFETIME

FREEDOM
IN OUR LIFETIME

The Collected Writings of Anton Muziwakhe Lembede

Edited by Robert R. Edgar

and Luyanda ka Msumza

Ohio University Press ■ *Athens*

Skotaville Publishers ■ *Johannesburg*

Mayibuye Books ■ *University of the Western Cape*

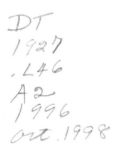
© Copyright by Robert R. Edgar and Luyanda ka Msumza
Published 1996 by Ohio University Press
Scott Quadrangle, Athens, Ohio 45701
Printed in the United States of America
All rights reserved
Ohio University Press books are printed on acid-free paper ∞

Library of Congress Cataloging-in-Publication Data

Lembede, Anton Muziwakhe, 1914-1947.
    Freedom in our lifetime : the collected writings of Anton
  Muziwakhe Lembede / edited by Robert R. Edgar and Luyanda ka Msumza.
      p.   cm.
    Includes bibliographical references and index.
    ISBN 0-8214-1149-7 (alk. paper)
      1. Blacks—South Africa—Politics and government.   I. Edgar,
  Robert R.   II. Msumza, Luyanda ka.   III. Title.
  DT1927.L46A2   1996
  968'.00496—dc20   96-7330
                                                                         CIP

Published in The Republic of South Africa
by Skotaville Publishers
Braamfontein, 2074, South Africa
and The Mayibuye Press
Mayibuye Books History & Literature Series No. 63
University of the Western Cape, Private Bag X17,
Bellville 7535, South Africa

The cover photograph has been reproduced with the permission of Bailey's African
History Archive

Quotation from *Long Walk to Freedom* by Nelson Mandela reproduced by permission of Little, Brown and Company. Copyright © by Nelson Rolihlahla Mandela.

To A. P. Mda (1917–1993)
Friend and Mentor

Contents

Religion and Churches

Debates and Relations with Other Organizations

Cultural Activities

Tributes to Lembede After His Death

Photographs

Acknowledgements

We first met each other in 1984 at A. P. Mda's law office in Mafe-teng, Lesotho, and we began a running conversation on South African society that continues to this day. We found that we shared an interest in Anton Lembede, so we decided to pool our resources and work on this collection. It has taken us many years to complete our task, but it has been an invaluable experience for both of us. And we have been assisted by and shared fellowship with many people along the way.

A number of people who knew Lembede have talked to us about their recollections. We wish to thank B. M. Khaketla, Victor Khomari, P. M. Gqobose, P. K. Leballo, Peter Borman, Joe Matthews, T. T. Let-laka, H. Moshoeshoe, Walter Sisulu, Albertina Sisulu, Ellen Kuzwayo, Edna Bam, Peter Raboroko, Mda Mda, Wycliffe Tsotsi, A. P. Mda, Rose Mda, Owen Mda, David Bopape, Victor Sifora, Nathaniel Ma-semola, and Godfrey Pitje.

We thank Colin Bundy, Tom Karis, Charles van Onselen, Karin Shapiro, Baruch Hirson, Michael West, Christopher Saunders, Peter Randall, Phil Bonner, and Patrick Furlong for commenting on our in-troduction to this volume. We are especially indebted to Gail Gerhart who not only commented on our introduction, but who repeatedly di-rected us to documents and shared transcripts from her own exten-sive collection of interviews. We have also benefitted from comments received at seminar presentations at the Institute of Social and Eco-nomic Research at Rhodes University; the Centre for African Studies at the University of Cape Town; and the Institute for Advanced Social Research at Witwatersrand University.

We also were assisted by various people and libraries who helped us locate information and people. These were Archbishop Denis Hurley; J. B. Brain; Rica Hodgson; Albert Grundlingh; A. H. Marais; Michele Pickering and Anna Cunningham of the C.P.S.A. Archive at Witwa-tersrand University; the South African Institute of Race Relations;

the State Library, Pretoria; the British Museum Newspaper Library; the South African Library, Cape Town; the Durban Daily News; and the Killie Campbell Library at the University of Natal, Durban.

We thank the Lembede family for sharing their family's history with us. We were overwhelmed by the hospitality they showed us when we visited the Lembede homestead in 1992. Mrs. Z. V. Cele and Patricia Lembede were particularly helpful in organizing our visit. We also want to express our thanks to Lembede's primary school teacher, Sister Bernadette Sibeko. We treasure the time we spent with her at Assisi Convent near Port Shepstone; and we are most grateful to her for sharing her photograph of Lembede's class that she kept for 65 years.

We dedicate this book to A. P. Mda. He dictated his foreword to this volume in 1992, a year before he died. He was an inspirational friend and mentor to both of us over the years.

We also wish to express our thanks to Walter Sisulu for contributing the other foreword. He reminds us of the vital role that youth play in renewing and challenging the old order, but his own example has taught us much about the virtues of experience, age, and wisdom.

Finally, we wish to thank the office of the Vice President for Academic Affairs at Howard University for financial assistance for a research trip in 1992.

Luyanda ka Msumza
Robert Edgar

Foreword

When I reflect on my memories of Lembede, two things stick out in my mind — his scholarliness and his innovative analysis of the freedom struggle. His dedication to his education brought him spectacular results. When he was young he got a lucky break. He had performed very brilliantly in Standard VI, so he was given a scholarship to further his education at Adams College. And he did well on that scholarship. He laid a good foundation for his later studies. He became a teacher, and this enabled him to work and earn some money — to support himself and his parents and prepare for his future.

He made rapid strides in his studies — all through self-study. Once he completed his B.A., he began working towards his LL.B., the Bachelor of Laws. And then he rounded off his education by earning an M.A. degree in Philosophy.

While he was studying and preparing for his thesis for his M.A. degree, we were staying together in Orlando East. We had extensive discussions because he was studying the philosophers from Descartes to the present day. Now that was very fortunate for me because he used to invite me to take part in discussing some of the issues raised by the philosophers. Very often we took opposite positions. I had to defend a certain position while he attacked it.

He wanted to gain some clearer understanding of the subject matter he was studying. He used me as a tool to achieve that goal. And, in this way, he also improved my knowledge. I was argumentative, too. I was a debater. I liked conflict, and he knew I was very stubborn. He was like that, too. He often challenged me. And after explaining to me so and so stood for this and that, he would make a reference to some book. He read to me, and I would read myself. Then we would discuss issues that he wanted to go deeper into. He invited me to take a certain line, an opposite line, so he could give me a chance to go deeper. He learned a lot from controversies because sometimes I attacked his positions just to give him an exercise in refuting my arguments.

When Lembede arrived in Johannesburg in 1943 to practice law, I was already there. In Orlando, I was chairman of the local branch of the ANC. There were people like myself and Walter Sisulu who had already been baptised into ANC politics, so we introduced him to the politics of Johannesburg and the ANC. But we soon learned that he was an independent and creative thinker; and he fast rose in the ranks of the young people who made up the Youth League.

Lembede was already politically conscious when he came to Johannesburg. He was critical of the set-up in South Africa — very critical. He could not understand why organisations like the ANC were weak. As time went on, it had become weaker and weaker. I likened the situation to a horse that was ridden by a small boy. The horse was not aware that it had greater powers than the boy. If it became aware, then it would not tolerate him for long. It would come to a point where the horse would say, "Get off. Get down quickly."

Now our power was potential. We weren't aware of it. Our power lay in the fact that we carried the South African society on our shoulders, literally in so far as our labour power was concerned. In the kitchens, in the gardens, in industry, on the roads, and on the farms, we more or less carried South Africa. However, our power was only imaginary. But if we could unite around some issue, we could go very far. Once we achieved unity, we would give our rulers an opportunity to change their line. Once we decided on positive action and we were united, we would truly shock the whole country. We did not want to destroy South Africa. We wanted people to change their views and decide to meet and compromise in discussion as human beings.

We were weak not only organisationally; we were weak in theory. We had not yet been able to study the situation in South Africa and the role we would play in bringing about a new South Africa. When Lembede and others joined the Youth League, we were quite clear on the general issues that faced us. But he was prophetic in his outlook; and this enriched his experience. He learned to come down to the people and to have the common touch and to address himself to the issues of common, ordinary poor people, workers and others. It was a great thing that he came amongst us. We really felt that he was a gifted man. He was learned. He had covered a lot of fields. He was a very clear thinker, a very good speaker. He came at a time when we needed a man of his type and background that enabled him to learn more and more and quickly.

He already had some clear-cut ideas on Africans. He was very critical of the African people. He said they were not conscious of who they were, where they came from, why they were here, and where they were going from here. Those were his complaints. It was our duty to devote ourselves to the great tasks of nation building along which we could lead the people and organise them. Very soon Lembede became accepted in the community and was acknowledged as a person who had a future in the country and would be useful to the people as a leader.

To those of us who personally knew Lembede he was an inspirational leader who left us as he was entering his most productive years. To present-day South Africans he is little more than a name from the past. I commend the editors for the patient detective work they have put into tracking down information on Lembede's life and collecting his writings. This volume will go far in educating people about Lembede, his ideas and politics. And I hope others will be challenged to follow its example and publish the writings of other stalwarts in our struggle. We need many more volumes like this so that present and future generations of South Africans can learn about their past and make their own critical judgments about what was said and done.

A.P. Mda

Foreword

I knew Anton Muziwakhe Lembede for only four years before his tragic and untimely death. But those four years were his most productive and significant — they were the years for which he is chiefly remembered.

From the first time when he came into my offices in Diagonal Street in 1943, Lembede struck me not only as a keen intellectual, but a philosopher and theoretician. He had an ability to examine ideas from any quarter, no matter how much he might diasgree with those who initiated them. He examined with rational interest, for example, the strategies used by Afrikaner nationalists to mobilise and uplift their poor — in those days there were many thousands of unskilled, jobless newcomers from the platteland. Lembede felt that Africans could learn from their successes. And from the communists, whom he firmly rejected both as a Catholic and an Africanist, he learnt to respect a militancy based on political theory (as opposed to the *hamba kahle* [go well] approach of the older ANC leaders). Lembede also reaffirmed the value of socialism as expressed in the precolonial African communal tradition.

It was Lembede, together with A. P. Mda and Nelson Mandela who sat up late at night drafting the political philosophy for an as-yet unborn Youth League, before presenting the document to colleagues such as Willie Nkomo, Lionel Majombozi, Oliver Tambo and myself, to consider and to critique. But of course Lembede, as a typical leader of the Youth League, fought the struggle not only politically, but with all the impressive skills at his disposal.

I remember clearly his practical support, as an articled clerk, together with Nelson Mandela, then a law student, in advising James Mpanza, head of the Sofasonke squatter movement, on how to challenge the Johannesburg Municipality on legal grounds to provide housing for the workers in the city. When the government wanted to deport Mpanza, Lembede together with Mandela, went to Pretoria to meet the Secretary for Native Affairs to argue the case against Mpanza's deportation.

It is not necessary to detail any further Lembede's passionate nationalism, his deeply spiritual nature and his earnest commitment to enhancing and promoting a mass-based African National Congress — these are well captured by Lembede's own words in this book.

Fifty years after the founding of the Youth League, the message of Lembede, its first elected president, remains clear: that it is the youth who have the capacity to renew the struggle, which today continues in a new form. It is the critical gaze of the youth who play the time-honoured role of re-examining the status quo, sometimes to the discomfort of the 'old guard.' It is they who have always had the capacity and the energy to renew and reinvigorate the ANC so that its grass-roots members could continue to play their rightful part in democratising our society. And, just as in Lembede's generation, the youth also have the flexibility to scrutinise their own positions, and have the courage to adapt them to changing conditions if need be. These are important lessons to examine in the context of Lembede's time, and to reconsider in the light of today's historic moment.

The editors of this book are to be congratulated for a timely and thoughtful tribute to an exceptional young man, for he played a key role in a turning point in the history of the ANC. This volume should be seen as a challenge to readers to collect the memories of others who participated in the struggle, who fought to take control of their lives and to mobilise others to do the same. The record of our political struggle still has a long way to go before present and future generations can fully appreciate and understand our past. Lembede's life is but one example of the remarkable courage and dedication that the forces of oppression and exploitation evoked in our people — old and young, men and women, black and white — to deepen and enhance the quality of the lives of all South Africans, in the time-honoured tradition of the ANC.

Walter Sisulu

Introduction

On Easter Sunday 1944 a group of young political activists gathered at the Bantu Men's Social Centre in downtown Johannesburg to launch the African National Congress Youth League (ANCYL). Motivated by their desire to shake up the "Old Guard" in the African National Congress (ANC) and set the ANC on a militant course, this "Class of '44" became the nucleus of a remarkable generation of African leaders: Nelson Mandela, Oliver Tambo, Walter Sisulu, Jordan Ngubane, Ellen Kuzwayo, Albertina Sisulu, A. P. Mda, Dan Tloome, and David Bopape. Many of them remained at the forefront of the struggle for freedom and equality in South Africa for the next half century.

However, the person the Youth Leaguers turned to in 1944 for their first president is not even listed in this group. He was a Natal-born lawyer, Anton Muziwakhe Lembede. Known to his friends as "Lembs," Lembede was a political neophyte when he moved from the Orange Free State to Johannesburg in 1943 to practice law. His sharp intellect, fiery personality, and unwavering commitment to the struggle made an immediate impression on his peers, and he was quickly catapulted into prominence in both the Youth League and the ANC. Though his political life was brief — he died tragically in 1947 — he left an enduring legacy for future generations. He is best remembered for his passionate and eloquent articulation of an African-centered philosophy of nationalism that he called "Africanism." A call to arms for Africans to wage an aggressive campaign against white domination, Africanism asserted that in order to advance the freedom struggle, Africans first had to turn inward. They had to shed their feelings of inferiority and redefine their self-image, rely on their own resources, and unite and mobilize as a national group around their own leaders. Though African nationalism remains to this day a vibrant strand of African political thought in South Africa, Lembede stands out as the first to have constructed a philosophy of African nationalism.

I

As South Africa enters a new era, we have decided to remember Lembede's contribution to the freedom struggle by assembling this collection of writings by and about him. Writing about Lembede is a challenging task for several reasons. One is that we are still faced with significant gaps in our knowledge of his life, especially the years before he moved to Johannesburg and entered politics. Another is that Lembede did not have the opportunity to develop many of his ideas fully because of the short time period in which he was politically active. Consequently, it is difficult to chart precisely the evolution of his political ideas. However, we believe this collection, which brings together Lembede's writings from his student days to just a few days before his death, significantly broadens our understanding of a seminal figure in South African political thought.[1]

We have divided this collection into eight sections. The first consists of essays he wrote in the 1930s when he was a student at Adams College and, later, a teacher in Natal and the Orange Free State. Subsequent sections present his political writings from 1944 to 1947 when he was active on the political scene and began to frame his philosophy of African nationalism. His views on African nationalism, religion, the ANC Youth League, cultural affairs, and other political movements were primarily set out in letters and essays he submitted to the black press. But we have also included reports on his speeches, a book review, excerpts from his M.A. thesis for the University of South Africa, and reactions to his activities and ideas. Finally, we have included tributes to Lembede by his contemporaries on his death.

EARLY LIFE AND EDUCATION

Looking back on his childhood days in Natal, Lembede was fond of telling his Johannesburg friends, "I am proud of my peasant origin. I am one with Mother Africa's dark soil." This declaration served a dual purpose: defining a political orientation and commitment and underscoring the fact that whatever his considerable educational, professional, and political achievements, he remained strongly attached to his rural roots.

Born on 21 January 1914 on the farm of Frank Fell at Eston, Muziwakhe Lembede was the first of seven children of Mbazwana Martin and Martha Nora MaLuthuli Lembede.[2] His father was a farm laborer who, according to his family, had a reputation among whites and blacks in his area for "listening, thinking . . . and . . . a quality of the fear of God which he impressed upon his children by deeds."

His mother attained a Standard V education (a considerable achievement for any African at that time) at Georgedale School and taught at schools at Vredeville, Darlington, and Umlazi Bridge. She tutored Anton at home in the basics of reading and writing until he was ready to pass Standard II. But she was anxious for him and her other children to escape their gruelling lives as farm laborers. Around 1927, she prevailed on her husband to relocate the family to Mphephetho in the Umbumbulu "native" reserve (situated mid-way between Pietermaritzburg and Durban) so that their children could have access to formal schooling.

The Lembede family history portrays their move to Umbumbulu as a positive search for educational opportunity, but it also coincided with a major upheaval on Natal's white farms. For a variety of reasons, white farmers evicted thousands of Africans from their farms in the late 1920s. Most of the dispossessed made their way to the urban areas or the overpopulated, overstocked, and unproductive African reserve areas that comprised roughly 7 percent of South Africa's land. Indeed, Lembede's father could not make ends meet on his plot of land at Mphephetho, and he had to supplement his income by working as a seasonal laborer on nearby white and Indian farms.[3]

Before the Lembede family moved to Umbumbulu, Muziwakhe, who had been baptized in the Anglican church and given the name Francis, converted to Catholicism and, with his father and brother Nicholas, joined a Roman Catholic church near Eston. The priest at Eston, Father Cyprian, gave Muziwakhe an additional name, Anton.

The church was to play a central role throughout Anton's life. As teenagers, he and Nicholas often played a game in which they acted out the role of a priest. Indeed, both told their family that they intended to become priests. However, Anton promised that before joining the priesthood, he would teach for a few years to pay school fees for his brothers and sisters.

Anton's formal education did not begin until he was 13, but he showed immediate promise in his classes. His teacher at the Catholic

Inkanyezi school was nineteen year old Bernadette Sibeko of Ladysmith, who was fresh out of Mariannhill Training College. Inkanyezi
was her first teaching post.

About 60 students squeezed into her classroom in a "building made
of wattle and daub with a corrugated iron roofing but with no ceil-
ing."[4] To Standard I and II students, she taught Zulu, English, hy-
giene, and scriptures. In addition, to Standard III and IV students, she
taught nature study, short stories from South African history, regional
geography and reading, writing, and arithmetic.

Sibeko was the sole teacher for all the classes, and one of her techniques for coping with such a large and diverse group of children was
to parcel out responsibilities. Since Anton was one of her best students, she often taught him a lesson and had him instruct the others.

Anton's dedication to his studies left distinct impressions on both
his family and Sibeko. His family remembers him herding the family
cattle, but being so engrossed by his books that he let the cattle
wander off. One of Sibeko's recollections was of watching him at a
football match, walking up and down a field in deep thought and occasionally kicking the ball when it came his way.[5]

On one occasion, Sibeko asked Anton to write an essay on money.
His response, written out on a slate with a pencil, so impressed her
that she copied it and entered it in a contest at a teachers' conference.
It was awarded first prize. When we interviewed her in August 1992,
she had no hesitation recollecting his short essay.

> Money is a small coin, a small wheel bearing the picture of the
> King's head. Round this head is an inscription — head of the
> King of England — George V. You can go to any store. If you
> present this coin the store-keeper gives you whatever you want.
> The nations know the value of money, and we too realise that
> money rules the world.

After Anton completed Standard III, Sibeko encouraged him to continue his education. He worked for a while in a kitchen at Escombe in
order to buy books and pay school fees at Umbumbulu Government
School, where he completed Standard VI with a first class pass. Then,
Hamilton Makhanya, a local school inspector, assisted him in secur-
ing a scholarship at nearby Adams College.

ADAMS COLLEGE

Established in 1849 to train African assistants to European missionaries, Adams College had by the 1930s become one of the premier schools for African students from all over southern and central Africa.[6] Adams had three divisions: a high school which took students through matriculation; an industrial school for training students in carpentry and building; and a teachers' training college, opened in 1909. A new teachers' course introduced in 1927 prepared students for the Native Teachers Higher Primary Certificate (later renamed the T3), which allowed a teacher to assume jobs in Intermediate Schools, High Schools, and Training Colleges. This was the course for which Lembede enrolled in 1933.

Lembede left indelible impressions on his classmates at Adams. First, there was his abject poverty which was apparent to everyone because of his shabby dress: his patched pants and worn-out jackets. Jordan Ngubane, a classmate and one of the founders of the ANC Youth League, described Lembede as the "living symbol of African misery."[7] Girls were embarrassed to be seen with him in public. Lembede was "very stupid in appearance," one female classmate recollected. "If any girl ever saw you, even if Antony [Anton] was innocently talking with you, then you'd become somebody to be talked about for the day."[8]

But there was another side of Lembede that his classmates consistently commented on, his brilliance and dedication to his studies. Edna Bam, who later taught in the faculty of education at the National University of Lesotho, drew a comparison of Lembede with J. E. K. Aggrey, the Ghanaian-born educator who had addressed an Adams audience in April 1921 when he visited South Africa as part of the Phelps-Stokes delegation investigating African education.[9] Aggrey was touted as the role model for all aspiring African students. Bam and other Adams students were told stories about Aggrey being so dedicated to his schooling that in the middle of winter he studied with his feet in a bucket of hot water. And that was the image that came to mind when she remembered Lembede.

Lembede excelled in learning languages. At Adams he picked up Afrikaans, Sesotho and Xhosa as well as German from German nuns residing near Adams, and he began studying Latin. Learning Afri-

kaans was even then regarded skeptically by African students. But
Ellen Kuzwayo recollected an occasion where Lembede spoke before a
group of students preparing for a debate with students at Sastri College, an Indian school in Durban. He started off his speech in English,
but then switched easily to Afrikaans.

In one of his student essays in the Adams' publication, *Iso Lomuzi*,
Lembede advised that the best way to learn new languages was to
combine the techniques of learning grammar with reading elementary readers.[10] In that same essay, he maintained that studying foreign
languages allowed one to understand other people and that contributed to lessening racial hatred. However, he also supported Africans
learning languages other than their own in order to put them in a
position to challenge whites who had established a monopoly over
African languages through their control of orthography and publications. "It speaks for itself," he stated, "that we want educated Bantu
men who have studied various Bantu languages, and who will be authorities on them."

Two other student essays, "The Importance of Agriculture" and
"What Do We Understand by Economics?", provide a glimpse into
Lembede's thinking on political and economic issues.[11] In them, he
placed the onus for black poverty on the African people themselves.
He charged that poor farming techniques and the laziness of African
farmers were directly responsible for their failures. Instead of drawing a connection between government policies and land shortages, he
faulted African farmers for reducing themselves to the level where
they had to seek work on white farms for a pittance. Lembede's own
father had been forced to supplement his family's income by periodi-
cally going out to work on the farms of neighboring white and Indian
farmers.

Lembede's solution was an education that taught people an appreciation for manual labor and applied modern agricultural techniques.
His role model was Booker T. Washington, the black American educator, whose ideas on industrial education and self-help had been
transplanted to Natal in the early twentieth century by an American-
trained Zulu, John Dube. Washington's principles permeated Dube's
own school, Ohlange Institute, and they had a significant impact on
the thinking of those in charge of African education throughout South
Africa in the following decades.

Lembede's student views are a pointed contrast to his criticisms of the government in the mid-1940s, but they highlight themes that consistently surface in his later writings — that Africans had to rely on their inner resources to overcome inequities and that spiritual beliefs were a necessary component of economic and political advancement.

The fact that Lembede's essays were not overtly political is not surprising since descriptions of Adams generally agree that the school did not have a politicized environment. Although Adams teaching staff included Albert Luthuli and Z. K. Matthews, who were to become prominent figures in the ANC, its administrators and teachers carefully insulated students from the political currents circulating about them. There was nevertheless one aspect of Adams that possibly influenced Lembede's nationalism of later years, a conscious effort on the part of Adams administrators to defuse ethnic tensions between students.

In this regard, a highlight of the school year was Heroes of Africa Day set aside to celebrate heroes of the African past. The campus had recognized Moshoeshoe Day and Shaka Day in the past, but when Edgar Brookes took over as Adams' principal in 1934, he created a Heroes' Day on 31 October, the eve of All Saints Day when "heroes" of the Christian faith were honored.[12] On Heroes' Day, students wore their national dress and gathered at an assembly to pay tribute to noted African figures from a culture other than their own. An Adams student, Khabi Mnqoma, has described the day's significance:

> The day is set aside to sing praises to heroes of South Africa, and to attempt to recapitulate the mode of life of our ancestors. As Adams College is what one might term cosmopolitan, the various students contribute towards drawing a picture of primitive African life.[13]

Ellen Kuzwayo recalls her feelings about the day:

> We crossed the tribal division on that day. . . . If I was Tswana, I had a freedom to depict my hero in another community in that cultural dress. Because I lived very near Lesotho, my grandfather's home . . . and I saw more of the Basotho people, saw their traditional dresses, their traditional dances, everything, and

I would be nothing but a moSotho. . . . And I think we didn't
realize it . . . but it kept us as a black community without saying, "You are Zulu. You are Tswana. You are Xhosa."[14]

TEACHING AND THE LAW

After leaving Adams in 1936, Lembede took up a series of teaching
posts, first at Utrecht and Newcastle in Natal and then in the Orange
Free State at Heilbron Bantu United School, where he taught Afrikaans, and Parys Bantu School, where he was headmaster.

His thirst for more education never stopped. Over the next decade
he steadily advanced himself through a series of degrees, all through
private study and financed with his meagre personal resources. He
passed the Joint Matriculation Board exams in 1937, taking Afrikaans
A and English B and earning a distinction in Latin. In 1940 he studied
for a B.A. degree, majoring in Philosophy and Roman Law, through
correspondence courses with the University of South Africa. He then
tackled the Bachelor of Laws (LL.B.) degree through the University of
South Africa, completing it in 1942. Finally, he registered for a M.A.
degree in Philosophy in 1943 at the University of South Africa, sub-
mitting his thesis entitled "The Conception of God as Expounded by,
or as it Emerges from the Writings of Philosophers — from Descartes to the Present Day" in 1945.[15] Considering the fact that only
a few Africans had attained graduate degrees, A. P. Mda's tribute to
Lembede on completing his M.A. was well-deserved: "This signal
achievement is the culmination of an epic struggle for self-education
under severe handicaps and almost insuperable difficulties. It is a
dramatic climax to Mr. Lembede's brilliant scholastic career."[16]

Lembede's ascetic lifestyle and his disciplined, austere study regi-
men were a major part of his educational success. According to B. M.
Khaketla, his roommate in Heilbron, Lembede would wake up at five
and read until six, when he prepared for school.[17] He taught from
eight until one. After lunch, at two, he came directly home and studied until seven o'clock when he broke for his evening meal. After
dinner, he studied until eleven. He followed this timetable religiously
on weekdays. On Saturdays, he read from five in the morning until

lunch. After lunch he read until he went to bed. Sundays he set aside for church, reading newspapers, and socializing.

Lembede also participated in the Orange Free State African Teachers' Association, an organization he scathingly censured in a letter to *Umteteli wa Bantu* (8 November 1941).

> Every year, many resolutions are adopted by the Conference. What is the fate of many of them? Some end just on the paper on which they are written. They are not acted upon, thus they fail to realise their ultimate destiny — action. . . . We must be action-minded. The philosophy of action must be the cornerstone of our policy. . . . In our ranks we have men and women of high talent and ability. Our poor, disorderly position is not occasioned by lack of talent, but (a) by lack of scientific organisation and utilisation of that talent, (b) by lack of will-power. Africans! Our salvation lies in hard and systematic work!

Never one to hold back his criticisms of African shortcomings, Lembede's impatience with the Association's inaction and lax discipline and his desire for positive action foreshadowed sentiments that made their way into his political views several years later.

Lembede also attended church services of the African branch of the Nederduits Gereformeerde Kerk (Dutch Reformed Church (DRC)), where he occasionally translated Afrikaans sermons into seSotho. Khaketla was struck by Lembede's fluency in both languages, and that he was willing to attend and appreciate services of denominations other than Catholic. His attitude was that "God is indivisible" and not subject to man-made divisions. He put on his best clothes and prepared himself for the monthly *nagmaal* services. Lembede thought *nagmaal* (Holy Communion) was more graceful and meaningful than the Holy Communion celebrated in the Catholic church; and he even chided Khaketla, an Anglican, that he could never understand the joy of *nagmaal* because Anglicans celebrated communion too frequently.

This is a pertinent anecdote because much has been made of Lembede's attachment to the Catholic church. Khaketla recollected that during one vacation, he went to Johannesburg and met Lembede by chance at Park Station. Lembede invited him to visit a friend, A. P.

Mda, in Orlando township. As they approached the Roman Catholic church in Orlando, they saw Mda in the churchyard. Khaketla recognized Mda because they had trained together as teachers at Mariazell school near Matatiele. Lembede asked Khaketla not to tell Mda that he had regularly attended DRC services in Heilbron. To Lembede, church affiliation did not mean as much as a belief in God. Moreover, participating in the DRC had partly been a tactic to get a job. He represented the DRC at Bantu United School, where every sponsoring denomination had to be represented on the staff.

An interesting sidelight of Lembede's stay in the Orange Free State was his search for a wife. According to his Parys roommate Victor Khomari, Lembede had a great reverence for educated women.[18] He vowed that he wanted to meet and marry the most brilliant woman he could find rather than confining himself to someone from within his own ethnic group. When he read in the press about a woman from Lesotho who had been a spectacular student at Morija Training College and the University College of Fort Hare, he decided to go to Mafeteng in Lesotho with Khomari on their school holiday. Khomari loaned him a bike to peddle to Thabana Morena, the school where the woman was teaching, but he was not able to meet her. By coincidence, the young woman in question, Caroline Ntseliseng Ramolahloane, later married B. M. Khaketla, Lembede's Heilbron roommate, in 1946.

One of Lembede's last acts before moving to Johannesburg was to contact J. D. Rheinallt Jones, director of the South African Institute of Race Relations, in June 1943 offering to do research for the Institute during the July vacation period. Rheinallt Jones asked Lembede to conduct a study of how African youths became "delinquents" by examining records of the Diepkloof Reformatory to determine how young people had run foul of the law. In accepting the offer, Lembede replied: "I think the work will be of some educative value to me also; and I hope my knowledge of Zulu, Sesotho, and Afrikaans will help me a lot in the investigation."[19] We do not have any record of the study that Lembede was commissioned to carry out, but his experience is probably reflected in the occasional comments on the deleterious impact of urban life on African youth that were woven into his political essays.

JOHANNESBURG

When Lembede had finished his LL.B. degree, he took up an offer to serve his articles with the venerable Pixley ka Seme, who had established one of a handful of African law firms in Johannesburg. After practicing law for over three decades, Seme was in poor health and on the verge of retirement, and he was looking for someone to take over his practice. His law career had had its less than distinguished moments. In 1932 he was struck from the roll of attorneys in the Transvaal, but was reinstated in 1942.[20]

He had also been a founding father of the ANC in 1912, and had served as its president from 1930 to 1937. A conservative, autocratic figure, Seme's presidency was marked by discord, and when he was ousted as president, he left the ANC at a low ebb. By the time Lembede began to work in his law firm, Seme was no longer a major player in ANC politics.

Whatever vicissitudes Seme had experienced in his legal and political careers, Lembede still held him in high regard. Moreover, because Seme was still a respected figure in the African community, he certainly eased Lembede's entry into African political and social circles.[21] In 1946, after Lembede had served his articles, Seme made him a partner in his firm. An Umbumbulu businessman, Isaac Dhlomo, loaned Lembede £500 to buy into Seme's firm.[22]

Lembede's law career was brief, but his linguistic abilities and his uniqueness as an African lawyer provided some memorable moments. One was when he shocked a magistrate in Roodepoort by conducting his case in Afrikaans. Another was when Lembede broke into Latin in a magistrate's court in Johannesburg, prompting the magistrate to interrupt and implore him: "Please, Mr. Lembede, this is not Rome, but South Africa."[23]

On another occasion Lembede appeared in a criminal case in a Pretoria court. The court officials were either unaware that there was a black attorney practicing or did not want to acknowledge him. So when Lembede arrived and informed the prosecutor that he was the attorney of record, the prosecutor brushed him off. Lembede responded by sitting in the public gallery. When his case was called, Lembede jumped up and announced from the gallery that he was appearing for the accused. The magistrate was taken aback by a person from the gallery claiming to be a lawyer and he called the prosecutor and Lembede into his chambers. Lembede came out to represent the defendant. The incident caused a stir among Africans in the gallery, primarily because Africans, too, were unaware that there were African attorneys, and because of the boldness of Lembede in challenging the prosecutor.[24]

After moving to Johannesburg, Lembede also renewed his friendship with A. P. Mda, whom he had first met in 1938 at a Catholic teachers' meeting in Newcastle. The two exchanged addresses, and when Lembede had occasion to visit Johannesburg, he would look up Mda. Born in 1916 in Herschel district near the Lesotho border, Mda had also received a Catholic education and earned his Teachers' Diploma at Mariazell. He moved to the Witwatersrand in 1937 and, after taking up a variety of jobs, he landed a teaching post at St. Johns Berchman, a Catholic primary school in Orlando Township. He rapidly rose to prominence in the Catholic African Union, the Catholic African Teachers' Federation, and the Transvaal African Teachers' Association. In the latter organization, he became a leading figure in the campaign to improve teachers' salaries and conditions of service.

He was also a veteran of African political organizations. He had been baptized into politics by attending the All African Convention (AAC) meeting in Bloemfontein in 1937. But he soon grew disenchanted with the AAC, and he moved into the ANC when it was revitalized in the late 1930s. Mda was clearly more politically experienced than Lembede. As Ngubane put it, living on the Witwatersrand had seasoned Mda as a political thinker and "as a result he had more clearly-defined views on every aspect of the race problem."[25]

For a while Mda and Lembede shared a house in Orlando. And as Lembede wrote his M.A. thesis, they became "intellectual sparring partners."[26] Mda sharpened Lembede's understanding of philosophical ideas by assuming opposing positions on issues and vigorously debating them with him. Mda was the perfect foil for Lembede because he loved the cut and thrust of debate, and he doggedly defended his positions with as much fervor as Lembede. Mda remembered their exchanges this way:

I had to defend a certain position while he attacked it. . . . He wanted to gain some clearer understanding of the subject matter he was studying. He used me as a tool to achieve that goal. . . . He learned a lot from controversies because sometimes I attacked his positions just to give him an exercise in refuting his arguments.[27]

In the same manner, the pair took on the major political questions of the day. There were occasions when Mda and other Youth Leaguers had to curb Lembede's instinctive bent to take extreme positions. When Lembede was living in the Orange Free State, in order to improve his command of Afrikaans, he began reading Hendrik Verwoerd's column, "Die Sake van die Dag," in *Die Transvaler,* the ultra-nationalist Afrikaans newspaper, and imbibing his ideas. As a result, after Lembede moved to Johannesburg, "Mda found Lembede rather uncritically fascinated with the spirit of determination embodied in fascist ideology, to the point where he saw nothing wrong with quoting certain ideas of Hitler and Mussolini with approval."[28] In the Orange Free State Lembede did not have the benefit of having peers around who could scrutinize and refine his thinking, but in Johannesburg, he had Mda and others who challenged him — not always successfully — to rein in some of his extremist ideas. For instance, Mda forced Lembede to rethink his fascination with fascism by pointing out Hitler's ideas about racial superiority and how they specifically applied to black people. By the close of the Second World War, Lembede was unequivocally rejecting fascism and Nazism in his writings.

Mda and Lembede found common ground on many political issues. And out of their discussions with each other and with their peers emerged a vision of a rejuvenated African nationalism — centered around the unity of the African people — that could rouse and lead their people to freedom.

THE FOUNDING OF THE ANC YOUTH LEAGUE, APRIL 1944

The years of the Second World War saw a quickening of the pace of African protest on the Witwatersrand.[29] The immediate cause of this ferment was the war itself, which disrupted trade flowing into South Africa. As a consequence, South Africa's manufacturing and mining sectors dramatically expanded to supply goods and arms for the allied war effort and for southern Africa. The economy boomed, and as white workers were siphoned off into the army, tens of thousands of African men and women, fleeing the stagnation of the rural areas, poured into the urban areas seeking jobs. Between 1936 and 1946, roughly 650,000 people moved into the urban areas. During those same years, Johannesburg's population leaped from 229,122 to 384,628, almost a 75 percent increase.

The wartime economy may have opened up employment opportunities for African workers, but at a cost. Prices of basic goods soared; housing shortages grew more acute; and municipalities charged higher prices for public transportation. White government and municipal officials did little to alleviate these burdens, and as a result, a series of protests — bus boycotts, squatter protests, and worker strikes — were triggered off in African townships throughout the Witwatersrand.

By and large, ANC leaders remained aloof from this protest. For the ANC the 1930s had been years of inaction and the All African Convention (AAC) had taken advantage of the ANC's lethargic leadership by eclipsing it as the pre-eminent vehicle for African opinion during and after the controversy over the Hertzog Bills. By the late 1930s, however, a group of activists, unhappy with the lack of direction and the compromises of AAC leaders, turned to resurrecting the ANC.

An important step in the ANC's revitalization was the election (by a slim majority of twenty-one to twenty) of Dr. A. B. Xuma as ANC president in 1940. Xuma, who had a flourishing medical practice in Johannesburg, rescued the ANC from its parlous economic condition by raising dues, soliciting donations from private sources, and contributing some of his own resources.

He also pushed through a new constitution in 1943, eliminating an Upper House of Chiefs. He toured throughout South Africa, imposing discipline and shoring up support among provincial ANC congresses. He opened a national office for the ANC in Johannesburg in December 1943. And he put the ANC in a position to respond to day-to-day situations by setting up a small working committee of people who lived within a fifty-mile radius around Johannesburg.[30]

There was no question of Xuma's commitment to equal political rights for Africans and the abolition of discriminatory laws, but he remained wedded to bringing about change through constitutional means. Although he was not at heart comfortable with mass protest and he was wary of the ambitions of younger ANC members, he understood that the ANC could not survive unless it brought younger members into its fold.

The inspiration for forming a Youth League came from several different quarters.[31] One influence came from the numerous youth and student organizations that had sprung up around the country. For instance, in 1939, Manasseh Moerane, principal of Umpumulo High School, and Jordan Ngubane, a journalist, founded the National Union of African Youth (NUAY) in Durban to promote literacy, economic and business training and political advancement for the African community. Without openly declaring it, they also intended to build an organization capable of breaking A. W. G. Champion's personal stranglehold over the Natal wing of the ANC.[32]

Several cohorts of future Youth Leaguers — Oliver Tambo, Congress Mbata, Lancelot Gama, William Nkomo, Nelson Mandela, Lionel Majombozi, James Njongwe and V. V. T. Mbobo — also emerged from the mid-1930s on at Fort Hare, the university college founded for African, Coloured and Indian students in 1916. By the Second World War several hundred students from all over southern Africa were studying for degrees at Fort Hare; and a number of them were intensely engaged in discussing and debating the political issues of the day: the abolition of the Cape African vote, the creation of a Natives Representative Council (NRC), the Italian invasion of Ethiopia, and the contest for global supremacy during the Second World War and its implications for Africans.

In the early 1940s Fort Hare students also received a bittersweet introduction to protest politics through their involvement in two strikes. The first was touched off in September 1941 after the white supervisor of the dining hall struck an African woman employee. Over three quarters of the students showed their sympathy with the worker by boycotting classes for three days. The Fort Hare administration had no sympathy for the strike and the issues raised by the students. They demanded that strikers submit a formal letter of apology for their actions and pay a fine of £1 or be suspended. All but one complied.

The second strike in September 1942 came about when Bishop C. J. Ferguson-Davie, the warden at Beda Hall, the residence for Anglicans, turned down a request by Beda students to play tennis on Sunday. When the majority of Beda students refused to cooperate with Ferguson-Davie in other activities such as chapel, he demanded that they sign a formal apology; if they did not they would be suspended from the university. Most of the students refused to sign the apology, and forty-five of the sixty-four Beda students, including Ntsu Mokhehle and Oliver Tambo, were suspended for varying periods of time.[33]

Another route to the Youth League was through the aggressive campaign of the Transvaal African Teachers' Association to improve the paltry wages and poor job conditions of black teachers. Teachers like A. P. Mda and David Bopape played prominent roles in educating and mobilising their communities behind the teachers' grievances. A high point of the teachers' protest was a march through downtown Johannesburg in May 1944 that reinforced a belief among its participants that militant resistance to the government could produce positive results. African teachers were to form a significant constituency in the Youth League.

A final factor that produced the Youth League was the challenge to the ANC by the newly-formed African Democratic Party (ADP), which featured two dynamic young leaders, Paul Mosaka and Self Mampuru. Mampuru had sought support from ANC youth when he considered standing for the presidency of the Transvaal ANC in 1943, but he had suddenly jumped to the ADP. Fearing the ADP would siphon off younger ANC members, Xuma cultivated relationships with youth leaders. And he responded positively when they proposed establishing a Youth League within the ANC.

Whatever their backgrounds, the common denominator for young ANC activists was their impatience with the unwillingness of the ANC "Old Guard" to adopt militant tactics to contest white rule. In the latter half of 1943 they began holding conversations on trains and at meetings at churches, the Bantu Men's Social Centre, and homes to discuss forming a youth wing in the ANC. A formal proposal to found a Youth League was put forward at the December 1943 meeting of the ANC in Bloemfontein, where pressing issues such as the approval of *Africans' Claims in South Africa,* a policy statement that spelled out ANC objectives as well as a Bill of Rights, and the relationship of the AAC and ANC were on the agenda. Youth leaders introduced and passed a resolution, proposed by Moerane and seconded by Mda, that stated: "henceforth it shall be competent for the African youth to organise and establish Provincial Conferences of the Youth League with a view of forming a National Congress of the Youth League immediately."[34]

After winning the blessing of Xuma, who overcame his misgivings about the ideas and roles of Youth Leaguers within the ANC, the Youth League issued its manifesto in March 1944 and held its inaugural meeting at the Bantu Men's Social Centre the following month.[35] Speakers included Lembede, Mda and V. V. T. Mbobo as well as senior Transvaal ANC leaders such as R. V. Selope Thema, E. P. Moretsele and Xuma. Youth Leaguers selected W. F. Nkomo and Lionel Majombozi, medical students at Witwatersrand University, as provisional chair and secretary, respectively, until the Youth League drafted a constitution and conducted a formal election for officers.

Nkomo and Majombozi enjoyed popularity among Youth Leaguers, but they were also selected because their status as medical students gave them the right educational credentials for senior ANC leaders such as Dr. Xuma. However, Nkomo and Majombozi were viewed as transitional appointments since it was known they would have little free time as students. In addition, Nkomo's leftist leanings troubled nationalists in the Youth League such as Mda and Lembede who believed Nkomo was secretly a member of the Communist Party of South Africa (CPSA). A tip-off, according to Ngubane, was Nkomo's suggested wording for the Youth League Manifesto "which in our opinion would have given it a slightly Communist slant."[36]

However, a political showdown was unnecessary. When Youth League elections took place in September, Nkomo stepped aside to concentrate on his studies. He remained a strong supporter of Youth League activities. Lembede was then elected first president of the Youth League, a position he held until his death.

Lembede had already begun making his mark on Youth League policy when Youth Leaguers delegated him, Ngubane, and Mda to draft the Youth League manifesto adopted in March 1944. Like Lembede, Ngubane was an Adams product and a newcomer to the Witwatersrand. He had been a reporter for John Dube's *Ilanga lase Natal* before moving to Johannesburg in 1943 to become an assistant editor at Selope-Thema's *Bantu World*. Ngubane, Lembede, and Mda were all Catholics and implacable opponents of the Communist Party.

The manifesto remains a classic statement of the African nationalist position. The conflict in South Africa, it asserted, was fundamentally a racial one between whites and blacks, who represented opposite political and philosophical poles. The oppressors, whites, represented a philosophy of personal achievement and individualism that fuelled fierce competition; the oppressed Africans embodied a philosophy of communalism and societal harmony where society's needs were favored over those of the individual. Because whites had defined their domination in terms of race, this had led the African "to view his problems and those of his country through the perspective of race."

The manifesto was also a blistering indictment of the orthodoxies that black and white leaders had been wedded to for decades. One was trusteeship, an idea promoted by white politicians that blacks were their wards who had to be brought along slowly to a civilized state. The manifesto surveyed the long litany of government laws that had hindered, not advanced Africans, and concluded that trusteeship was a bluff aimed at perpetuating white rule.

Another orthodoxy was the belief of ANC leaders that change could come through compromise and accommodation. The Youth Leaguers charged that senior ANC leaders had grown remote and aloof from the African community and were trapped between their apprehensions over losing the few privileges the government granted them and their qualms over mass African protest bringing down the wrath of the government. The result was that ANC leaders had become "suspicious of progressive thought and action" and offered no innovative policies or strategies for combatting "oppressive legislation." They were so locked into segregationist structures such as the Natives Representative Council (NRC) that they had drifted away from the ANC's original vision and vitality.

The manifesto's criticisms of ANC leadership were devastating, but rather than calling on people to defect from the ANC, it invited Youth Leaguers to remain loyal and serve as "the brains-trust and power-station of the spirit of African nationalism" and infuse the ANC with a new spirit. The manifesto's political goals were clear:

self-determination and freedom for the African people. But other than calling for a radical reversal of ANC policies, the manifesto did not clearly spell out alternative strategies. That tactical omission was not addressed until after Lembede's death, when Youth Leaguers launched their drive to pressure the ANC to adopt a Programme of Action.

That Lembede was a relative newcomer to Johannesburg and politics did not hamper his rapid rise to prominence in the Youth League and the parent ANC. This can be attributed to several factors. One was that he was a lawyer, serving his articles with Seme, and thus in a prestigious position looked upon favorably by the ANC "Old Guard," who did not treat anyone seriously who lacked education or status. Another was that Lembede had completed his legal studies and was in a profession relatively immune to direct government pressure. Many of the Youth Leaguers were teachers, and they, like Moerane, had to tread cautiously when it came to their political activism.

Moreover, there was no question of Lembede's leadership qualities and his zealous devotion to Youth League causes. A tenacious debater and a stirring orator, he showed no hesitancy in staking out contentious positions and promoting them fearlessly in any setting and against any adversary. Even within the Youth League, which had a strong left-of-center faction, Lembede had to defend his Africanist positions against charges that they were too extreme. Congress Mbata recollected: "He was almost alone and he fought a very brave battle; I must say we respected him for his stand. He was a man who if he was convinced about a thing would go to any length to make his viewpoint."[36]

Whatever reservations Youth Leaguers had with Lembede's ideas and his lack of grounding in practical politics, they recognized that he was willing to take on any challenge, no matter how much opposition it provoked. An example was Lembede's call for African leaders to boycott the NRC, set up by the government in 1937. The government never intended the NRC to be more than an advisory board, but conservative and moderate African leaders (including some prominent ANC officials), hoping to exploit the NRC as a platform for expressing African opinion, decided to participate. However, the NRC never became more than an irrelevant talk-shop.

To Youth Leaguers, the real issue was full political rights for Africans, and they appealed to African leaders to refrain from participating in NRC elections. In the aftermath of the 1946 mine workers strike, Lembede introduced a resolution at the ANC national conference calling on NRC members to resign immediately. However, most senior ANC leaders, including prominent Communists, argued that a boycott would not succeed unless there was unanimity about the strategy within the African community. Otherwise, some African politicians would participate in the NRC and do the government's bidding. When Lembede's resolution was overwhelmingly defeated, it was further proof to the Youth Leaguers of how out of touch ANC leaders were with the militant mood in the African community. "The masses are ready to act," Lembede challenged the ANC national executive, "but the leaders are not prepared to lead."[37]

Although Lembede's stances provoked harsh reactions, he never shied away from controversy. Indeed he seemed to revel in it. Mda recalled a meeting in Orlando where he and Lembede shared a platform. Lembede thought the meeting was not lively enough, so he deliberately stirred things up by launching an attack on the Communist Party. This meeting, according to Mda, provoked a ferocious response from the Communist Party newspaper *Inkululeko*. Quoting an eyewitness at Lembede's speech, *Inkululeko* reported: " 'He spoke firmly but like a qualified Nazi. In fact if one were to close one's eyes, one would certainly think one was listening to Hitler broadcasting from Berlin.' "[38]

Joe Matthews recounted another occasion where Lembede and Mda were invited to address the debating society in the geography room at St. Peter's School where Youth Leaguers Oliver Tambo and Victor Sifora were teaching.

> So Lembede got up, and he was dressed . . . in a black tie, black evening dress, which in itself was quite something. And he started off, "As Karl Marx said, 'A pair of boots is better than all the plays of Shakespeare.' "

This provocative statement roused his predominantly student audience, but it also prompted a sharp retort from the school's geography teacher, Norman Mitchell, a devotee of the British Empire, who angrily shouted back, "That's not true."[39]

A PHILOSOPHY OF AFRICAN NATIONALISM

In South Africa, "nation" and "nationality" have been elastic concepts whose boundaries expand or contract according to the relative power or powerlessness of those defining them. A case in point is Lembede, whose starting point for his vision of African nationalism was his recognition of a fundamental political reality: that as long as Africans did not transcend their ethnic divisions, they would remain minor political actors. Unless the continent's millions of inhabitants agreed to work cooperatively, Africans could not hope to take advantage of global power shifts and compete with established powers such as the United States, Japan, Germany, Russia, England, and France and newly emerging ones such as China and India. Moroever, in South Africa, where white domination was perpetuated by dividing the African majority, African unity — based on a shared oppression — was a precondition for challenging the status quo.

Because Lembede's brand of nationalism was aimed at forging a pan-ethnic identity, he discounted the usual building blocks of nationalism. What bound the peoples of Africa together and made them unique was not language, color, geographical location or national origin, but a spiritual force he called "Africanism." This concept first appeared in his writings in 1944, and was based not only on the fact that Africans shared the same continent but that they had adapted to Africa's climate and environment. "The African natives," he contended, "then live and move and have their being in the spirit of Africa, in short, they are one with Africa."[41]

Borrowing liberally from Darwin's law of variation in nature, Lembede maintained that because nations differed in the same way as flowers, animals, plants, and humans, they had special qualities and defining characteristics. Accordingly, Africa had to "realise its own potentialities, develop its own talents and retain its own peculiar character."[42]

This deterministic line of reasoning had a kinship with the neo-Fichtean ideas then being advanced by some Afrikaner nationalists. Lembede was certainly familiar with their writings through the Afrikaans press and his M.A. research. In his thesis, he quoted from a booklet on communism by Nicolaas Diederichs, a professor of Political Philosophy at the University of the Orange Free State and a Broe-

derbond leader.[43] Lembede's ideas mirrored aspects of Diederichs'
philosophy of nationalism, presented in his *Nationalisme as Lewens-
beskouing en sy verhouding tot Internasionalisme* (1935). For instance,
the unifying characteristic of Diederichs' nationalism was not "a common fatherland, common racial descent, or common political convictions," but a divinely ordained "common culture."

> Just as He ruled that no deadly uniformity should prevail in na-
> ture, but that it should demonstrate a richness and variety of
> plants and animals, sound and colors, forms and figures, so in
> the human sphere as well He ruled that there should exist a
> multiplicity and diversity of nations, languages and cultures.[44]

No doubt Lembede appropriated some of the ideas of Afrikaner
nationalists for his version of African nationalism. While Afrikaner
nationalists distorted evolutionary theory to justify white domination,
Lembede probably took special delight in recasting the same ideas to
promote African equality with Europeans. Moreover, his concept of
African nationalism was fundamentally opposed to Afrikaner nationalism. This is illustrated by a story Jordan Ngubane related to Mary
Benson about Lembede having a meeting with a leader of the *Ossewa
Brandwag* (OB), an ultra-nationalist Afrikaner movement. The OB
leader told Lembede that "we Afrikaner nationalists realise that no nationalist is an enemy of another nationalist. We have much that is common, land, you are exploited by Jews, English, and Indians just as we
are by Jews and English, we know that you are suffering and in final
record [the] only real friend of a nationalist is another nationalist. We
want to make a gesture of friendship." The OB leader then allegedly
handed Lembede a £500 check to be used as Lembede saw fit as a gesture of "goodwill towards African nationalists." Lembede expressed
his appreciation but pointed out that the "goals of Afrikaner and African nationalism [are] irreconcilable therefore [it is] unfair to you and
me if I accepted help from your side." Lembede then walked away.[45]
    Because Lembede did not accept that ideas and innovations were
bound by culture, he saw no inconsistency in taking ideas from non-
Africans to construct an Africa-centred philosophy. Thus his writings
drew on an electic range of sources: nineteenth century European
romantic nationalists, Greek and Roman philosophers, and leaders of

Indian, Egyptian, and other anti-colonial struggles. He valued the contributions of Western and Eastern civilizations and he argued that Africa was ideally placed to absorb the best from both. However, he warned against uncritically borrowing ideas that had no application to the African continent.[45]

Lembede's ideas clearly were Pan African in scope, but it is striking that at no point in his writings did he refer to the Pan African Congresses or any of the leading lights of Pan Africanism. Lembede's ideas, for instance, echo those of Edward Wilmot Blyden, the West Indian/Liberian educator and philosopher who wrote on the creative and distinctive genius of the "Negro" race and the necessity for Africans to express racial pride and forge a unified nationality. Also curiously absent from Lembede's writings is any mention of Marcus Garvey, the Jamaican-born black nationalist. Garvey's ideas had not only caught hold in the United States after the First World War, but had also attracted a fervent following in South Africa. There is ample oral evidence that Lembede was familiar with Garvey since Lembede frequently peppered his speeches with quotations from *The Philosophy and Opinions of Marcus Garvey,* but we do not have an explanation why Lembede did not cite Garvey in his writings.[46]

Lembede is most commonly associated with the framing of a philosophy of African nationalism, but one cannot separate his ideas from the political ends they served. One objective was to create an ideological arsenal for African nationalists in the ANC to wage combat with their principal political rivals, who had staked out clearly-defined doctrines and policies. For instance, the Communist Party of South Africa was rooted in Marxist dogma and regularly issued policy statements. The Non-European Unity Movement, which had an influential Trotskyite wing, had its 10-Point Programme (a central plank was the boycott of government-created institutions), ratified in December 1943. And the African Democratic Party, touting a multiracial membership, had adopted its manifesto in September 1943 advocating change through peaceful negotiation and opposing militant protest. African nationalists were at a disadvantage in proselytizing their cause unless they translated their emotions, aspirations and convictions into a logical and coherent set of doctrines independent of European ideologies. In the battle of the "isms," the Youth League could put forward "Africanism" as an alternative.

In order for Africans to combat white domination, Lembede maintained they had to overcome psychological disabilities. The system of segregation had erected tangible political and economic barriers that were easily targeted, but white domination also had a corrosive impact on the self-image of Africans, and this was more difficult to cope with. This negative self-image was manifested in Africans' "loss of self-confidence, inferiority complex, a feeling of frustration, the worship and idolisation of whiteness, foreign leaders and ideologies."[47] According to Lembede,

> . . . the African people have been told time and again that they are babies, that they are an inferior race, that they cannot achieve anything worthwhile by themselves or without a white man as their "trustee" or "leader." This insidious suggestion has poisoned their minds and has resulted in a pathological state of mind. Consequently the African has lost or is losing the sterling qualities of self-respect, self-confidence and self-reliance. Even in the political world, it is being suggested that Africans cannot organise themselves or make any progress without white "leaders."
>
> Now I stand for the revolt against this psychological enslavement of my people. I strive for the eradication of this "Ja-Baas" mentality, which for centuries has been systematically and subtly implanted into the minds of the Africans.[48]

Lembede's ultimate cure for these ills was political freedom, but he prescribed several intermediate steps which Africans could take to reassert an independent identity. One was reversing the distorted image of their own past. This meant constructing a history that accentuated the positive achievements of African civilizations, praising the heroic efforts of African leaders who resisted European expansion and resurrecting the glories of the African past. Influenced by Seme, Lembede's historical vision drew a linear connection between present and past African civilizations, going back to ancient Egypt.

> The roots of civilisation are deep in the soil of Africa. Egypt is the cradle of civilisation not only in the sciences but even in the matter of sharing. Hannibal, conqueror and polygamist, had three black African wives; Moses married an African; neither

Europe nor Asia is devoid of African blood. Christ himself, at a young age, found protection in Africa. On His way to Calvary his support came from Africa.[49]

Lembede had no tolerance for anyone who presented a contrary view of Africans and their history. Reviewing B. W. Vilakazi's novel, *Nje-Nempula,* situated during the Bambatha rebellion, Lembede reproached Vilakazi for casting Malambule, a collaborator in Lembede's eyes, as a lead character because it might "sew [sic] the seed of a defeatist mentality or an inferiority complex in the minds of our children."

> we should not tell our children that we were routed, humiliated and cowed by white people, we should merely tell them that in the face of superior force and weapons, we were compelled to lay down arms. . . . The motto of a National hero should be 'My people, right or wrong.'[50]

Lembede also called on Africans to break their reliance on European leaders and ideas by building up their own organizations. A key to this strategy was making the ANC and African leadership central to the African national struggle. In this regard, Lembede did not operate in a world of political ambiguity. He set down clearly defined lines of demarcation between the ANC and other organizations. He spurned appeals to ethnicity; he promoted African national unity over class identities; and he rejected Africans merging their cause with other "non-European" groups and sympathetic whites.

For instance, he dismissed the prospect of "Non-European unity" — combining African, Coloured, and Indian political organizations into one movement — as "a fantastic dream" because they were split along the lines of national origin, religion, and culture as well as by their relative positions in the pecking order of segregation.[51]

Lembede took a rigid and narrow view of Indians: they were merchants who fought "only for their rights to trade and extract as much wealth as possible from Africa." His analysis was a gross simplification of the Indian community's class composition. Although leaders of Indian political movements were professionals, who came from better-off families, most Indians were industrial workers and farm laborers.

Lembede's stance towards Coloureds was more flexible. He recognized that Coloureds were an arbitrarily defined group with many divergent attitudes and positions. Therefore, he welcomed into the African national movement Coloureds who "identified themselves and assimilated into African society," but he excluded those who classified themselves as a separate nation or as Europeans and those who shared the racist attitudes of Europeans towards Africans.

Lembede also argued that, in the hierarchy of segregation, Indians and Coloureds benefitted from an "inequality of oppression" that accorded them slight privileges closed off to Africans. If Indian and Coloured leaders were put in a position to advance their own political and economic interests, Africans could not realistically expect them to side with African causes.

One of the likely sources for Lembede's attitude was the events surrounding the passage of Hertzog's Representation of Natives Act (1936), which abolished the Cape African vote. Although Coloured and Indian leaders had joined Africans in founding the All African Convention in 1935 to protest the law, a perception developed among some Africans that the commitment of Coloured and Indian political leaders had significantly diminished once the threat to their own status had eased.[52]

Despite Lembede's reservations about Non-European unity, he recognized that there were grievances such as voting rights on which African, Coloured, and Indian political movements could find common ground. In those cases, he urged political movements to confer with each other and arrive at joint strategies for addressing issues. Thus, after being brought onto the ANC executive in 1946, he supported moves towards closer cooperation between the ANC and the Natal and Transvaal Indian Congresses.

Another Lembede tenet was that since Africans were discriminated against because they were Africans, preserving their national unity overrode any class divisions within the African community. Therefore, the handful of Africans who had acquired wealth were not excluded from the national struggle because they had not been co-opted "into the ranks of and society of white capitalists."

A corollary was that African workers should align their struggles with the ANC rather than pursuing an elusive class unity with workers from other racial or ethnic groups. African workers were oppressed not as workers, but as a race, by an alliance of white capitalists and a white Parliament which had legislated a labor aristocracy for Europeans (and Indians and Coloureds to a lesser degree) who profited from higher wages and access to better jobs.[53]

Lembede viewed the struggles of African workers as legitimate in their own right and a vital component of ANC activities. The "A.N.C. without a workers' organization (like the I.C.U. [Industrial and Commercial Workers' Union])," he conceded, "is a motionless cripple." He backed the efforts of African workers to join trade unions and fight for higher wages and improved working conditions. However, he believed the aspirations of both black trade unions and the ANC were best served by forging a joint strategy, with trade unions dealing with economic issues and the ANC concentrating on political matters. His reference in the above quote to the ICU is significant because of the lesson he drew from the destructive rivalry of the ANC and the ICU in the 1920s — that their competition had led to the ICU's dramatic collapse and the precipitous decline of the ANC until its revitalization during the Second World War.[54]

Throughout his career, Lembede was consistently hostile to the Communist Party on religious and racial grounds. As a devout Christian, he rejected Communism's materialist ideas as alien to the African experience. He had studied some of the classic works of Marxism while writing his M.A. thesis and he took issue with the materialist argument that advances in modern science and knowledge were antithetical to religious beliefs. Moreover, he questioned the materialist contention that Christianity lulled Africans into political passivity. Instead, he pointed to Christian ministers who had been fixtures in the ANC's leadership since its inception and he maintained that Christianity could be a spur to political action. Anticipating the liberation theologians, he interpreted the Christian message — especially the symbolism of Christ's crucifixion — as a revolutionary creed capable of mobilizing people to action. "The essence of Christianity," he maintained, "is Calvary; or the Cross — the ready willingness to offer and sacrifice one's life at the altar of one's own convictions, for the benefit of one's followers."[55]

As an African nationalist, Lembede was alarmed by the growing

prominence of Communists in the ANC and other organizations.
Like the ANC, the Communist Party had resurrected itself in the late
1930s and had rapidly expanded its membership by aligning itself
with popular struggles in the black community, especially in the urban areas, organising trade unions, launching a national anti-pass
campaign, and actively involving itself in ANC affairs. By 1945 the
ANC national executive had three communists on it; and Lembede
had concluded that Communists were the Youth League's most serious rival for the activist wing of the ANC.

That same year, Lembede and the Youth League pressed the Transvaal ANC to adopt a resolution stating that members of the ANC national or provincial executives could not belong to other political
organizations.[56] The resolution, directed specifically at Communists
on the ANC executive, was aimed at forcing them to declare their allegiance to the ANC or the Communist Party. The resolution passed
thirty-one to twenty-four. But when it was considered by the national
body, it was rejected. Although Dr. Xuma and other senior ANC
leaders were clearly not wild-eyed radicals, they viewed the ANC as
an umbrella group composed of many different constituencies and
they objected to an ideological litmus test for ANC membership.[57]

Lembede was wary of African communists, but he was particularly
suspicious of the motives of white Communists assuming leadership
roles in African organizations, especially trade unions, because he believed their presence undermined African leaders and fragmented African unity. In 1945, Lembede's Transvaal Youth League turned down
an invitation to affiliate with the Progressive Youth Council (linked
to the Communist Party). Writing to Ruth First, the Council's secretary, the Youth League declared that it could not subordinate itself to
any other youth organization, especially when there was "a yawning
gulf between your policy or philosophic outlook and ours."[58]

Lembede was certainly an uncompromising foe of the Communist
Party, but was he categorically opposed to all socialist ideas? In this
area at least, his writings are open to debate as to where his thinking
was headed. In one essay, he promoted a variant of African socialism,
arguing that since precapitalist African societies held land commu-
nally, they were "naturally socialistic as illustrated in their social practices and customs." His ideas were in line with other proponents of

African socialism who stressed the classless harmony and unity of African societies before Europeans came on the scene. There are only a few hints in his writings of a critical assessment of capitalism and its implications for African societies. However, in one essay, he noted that since African socialism was a "legacy" to be tapped, "our task is to develop this socialism by the infusion of new and modern socialistic ideas."[59] He did not define just what these ideas were, but he was very clear that national liberation had to precede any implementation of socialist ideas, however they were defined.[60]

LEMBEDE'S DEATH

By 1947, having completed his education and having settled into his law practice, Lembede was poised to further his professional and political ambitions. And, after many years of personal privation, he was finally in a position to look after his family's welfare. He began sending money to his widowed mother; he paid *lobola* (bridewealth) for his brother Alpheus; and he promised his sister Cathrene and her husband, Alpheus Makhanya, that he would bring one of their children to Johannesburg and pay for his education.

He was also re-establishing his roots in Umbumbulu. He built a four room house for himself at the Lembede homestead. He bought a Buick and instructed his family to begin building a road to his new home.[61] His last letter home read:

> Mame,
>   Sengithenge imoto enowayilensi. Ngiyofika ngayo lapho ekhaya. Makumbiwe umgwaqo uze ungene ekhaya. Ngizothumela u £20 wokumba umgwaqo.
> [Mother,
>   I have now bought a car with a wireless [radio]. I will be driving next time I come home. You must dig the road until it reaches home. I will be sending £20 for this purpose.][62]

And he was finalizing arrangements for marriage to 24-year old Cherry Mndaweni, a nurse trained at McCord Hospital in Durban. The two had met sometime in 1945 on a bus going from Ladysmith to nearby Driefontein, Mndaweni's birthplace, where Lembede was han-

dling a legal case. According to her, it was love at first sight; and after
Lembede returned to Johannesburg, they started writing letters to
each other. What made Lembede so appealing to her was his spiritual
nature and his concern with family issues. She also recognized that
Lembede felt comfortable with her because she had grown up in a
rural area and had not taken on urban ways. Her membership in the
Methodist church made no difference to him, but she expected to
convert to Catholicism after they married.

After finishing her training at McCord, she moved to Germiston to
be closer to him. She heard from friends that he was involved in politics, but she was still puzzled when he told her that when he was arrested one day she would have to take care of their children. She only
understood the meaning of his remark as the political struggle intensified in the 1950s.

Their marriage plans moved forward in 1947 when he visited her
father, a clerk at the Cimmaron Jack mine in Germiston to initiate
discussions on *lobola*. He also delegated several friends to visit her
family at Driefontein to finalize arrangements. However, he post-
poned his own planned visit to Driefontein in order to serve as master of ceremonies at a reception on Sunday 26 July celebrating the
awarding of a B.A. degree to his treasured friend, A. P. Mda.[63] Mda
had decided to follow in Lembede's footsteps and pursue a law career;
he left the next day to return to his temporary teaching post at Pius
XII College in Roma, Basutoland.

On the morning of 27 July, Lembede fell ill at his law office. Both
Nelson Mandela and Walter Sisulu have claimed that they were passing by his law office and noticed Lembede doubled over in pain on his
couch.[64] They and Lembede's clerk called on Dr. S. Molema for assistance, and Lembede was taken to Coronation Hospital where he died
on Wednesday, 29 July 1947, at 5:30 a.m. The cause of death was listed
as "cardiac failure" with "intestinal obstruction" a contributing factor.
Lembede's abdominal complications were longstanding. He had nearly
died from an operation in 1940 for abdominal problems and he had
had a similar operation in 1941.[65]

Lembede's last words, taken down by his attending nurse Rabate,
were characteristically directed to his family:

All the money must be given to Nicholas, and he should use this money for going to school with. He should look well after my mother because I am taking the same path which my forefathers took. And the clothing should be given to my brother . . . and he should try and do all the good in order to lead the African nation. God bless you all.[66]

Lembede was laid to rest at Croesus cemetery on 3 August.[67] His pallbearers and speakers represented a broad spectrum of black political and educational leaders: Pixley ka Seme, Elias Moretsele, Oliver Tambo, Templeton Ntwasa, Hamilton Makhanya, Yusuf Dadoo, A. P. Mda, Obed Mooki, Sofasonke Mpanza, Jordan Ngubane, A. B. Xuma, William Nkomo, Paul Mosaka and B. W. Vilakazi. Lembede may have been an intense competitor in politics, but he rarely allowed that to stand in the way of developing strong friendships with his political rivals.

Following Lembede's death, Mda took over as acting president of the Youth League until he was formally elected president in early 1948. Although he and Lembede are often paired as the Romulus and Remus of African nationalism, they did have differing visions of nationalism. Mda's views were not as "angular" as Lembede's; he was uncomfortable with some of Lembede's extreme stances. Although he agreed with Lembede that there was a major gulf between Africans, Coloureds, and Indians that could not be bridged in the short run, he had long argued that African nationalism "must not be the narrow kind, the unkind kind that discriminated against other racial groups." He desired "a broad nationalism, imbued with the spirit of Christ's philosophy of life and recognising the universal brotherhood of men."[68] After he became Youth League president, he elaborated on this point in a letter he wrote to Godfrey Pitje, a lecturer at Fort Hare and Mda's successor as Youth League president:

Our Nationalism has nothing to do with Fascism and Nationalism [sic] Socialism (Hitleric version) nor with the imperialistic and neo-Fascist Nationalism of the Afrikaners (the Malanite type). Ours is the pure Nationalism of an oppressed people, seeking freedom from foreign oppression. We as African Na-

tionalists do not hate the European — we have no racial hatred:
— we only hate white oppression and white domination, and not
the white people themselves! We do not hate other human beings as such — whether they are Indians, Europeans or Coloureds.[69]

In drafting the Youth League's *Basic Policy,* adopted in 1948, Mda
took the occasion to incorporate these views as well as distance the
Youth League from some of Lembede's radical positions. Mda in-
serted a section, "Two Streams of African Nationalism," in which he
rejected the one variant of African nationalism identified with

> Marcus Garvey's slogan — 'Africa for the Africans.' It is based
> on the 'Quit Africa' slogan and on the cry 'Hurl the Whiteman
> to the sea.' This brand of African Nationalism is extreme and
> ultra revolutionary.[70]

Because Lembede often referred to Garvey in his speeches, this was a
subtle way for Mda to signal a departure from some of Lembede's positions.

Mda also moved to strengthen the organizational network of the
Youth League by traveling to all the provinces to shore up existing
chapters, start new ones, and cultivate established ANC leaders. By
then Mda was operating from his birthplace, Herschel district, where
he was teaching, so he developed his most extensive network in the
eastern Cape. The Youth League's most energetic chapter was at Fort
Hare, where there was already a group of students and staff receptive
to the message of African nationalism.

In addition, Mda was a key figure in lobbying the ANC to adopt a
militant Programme of Action. The impetus for the Programme came
in the aftermath of the Nationalist Party's election victory in May
1948. At its December conference later that year, the ANC passed a
resolution supporting the drafting of a programme of action to combat the new government and its avowed apartheid policies. Over the
next year, Mda and other Youth Leaguers worked with senior ANC
leaders to fashion a statement that committed the ANC to combat
apartheid with a range of weapons: boycotts, strikes, work stoppages,
civil disobedience and non-cooperation. The ANC approved the Programme of Action at a tumultuous conference in December 1949.

At the same time as Mda was putting the Youth League on a different footing, he also tried to memorialize Lembede's ideas so that the nationalist position would continue to be promoted within the ANC and win new converts. Mda lectured on Lembede from time to time, but formal Lembede commemorations did not get off the ground until the mid-1950s.[71] Promoting Lembede's views became critical after 1949 as the ANC (and Youth Leaguers) began to split into two camps — those who retained their commitment to a "pure" African nationalism and those who were prepared to forge alliances with political organizations representing other racial groups and the Communist Party. The former, clustered in a group named the "Africanists," were the nucleus of the faction that eventually broke away from the ANC to form the Pan Africanist Congress (PAC) in 1959. The Africanists also held Lembede memorials and used their journal, *The Africanist,* to reprint some of his essays as well as tributes to him and his ideas.

CONCLUSION

"No man outside the lunatic asylum can shamelessly maintain that present leaders are immortal. They must, when the hour strikes, inexorably bow down to fate and pass away, for: 'There is no armour against fate, Death lays his icy hand on Kings.'" When Lembede penned these words in early 1947, he was not anticipating his own death seven months later, but the inevitable transfer of leadership from one generation to another. However, the fact that his life was cut short before he realized his full potential inevitably influences the way in which people view his contribution to South African political life.

A parallel that people often turn to is the Old Testament story of the Israelite search for the promised land. At a Lembede memorial held in mid-1955, a prominent African Methodist Episcopal minister, Nimrod Tantsi, compared Lembede to Moses who "led the Israelites out of Egypt and died before reaching Canaan," and he appealed for new Joshuas to step forward to lead Africans to their freedom.[72] In 1992, when we asked A. P. Mda to reflect on Lembede's contributions, he used the analogy of Moses not only to describe Lembede, but also to reinforce a point that Lembede repeatedly stressed about the importance of African leadership in the freedom struggle.

A leader of the African people must come from the Africans themselves. A true leader who's going to lead them to their freedom. . . . Moses belonged to the Jewish people, the Israelites. . . . He gave them the direction. They followed that path which he gave them. In this situation the road to salvation is this one. Let's be together, gather our forces, and then march forward and cross the Red Sea. There can be no freedom unless we cross the Red Sea. We can cross the Red Sea only if we, the Israelite leaders, lead you because we are part and parcel of you — we see the way as you see it. And we've got a clear vision of where we can go. . . . Moses is part of you. He is yourselves. And he can lead you through the dangers of the Red Sea and the desert and march in unity across the desert facing all the difficulties until we end up in the promised land.[73]

Lembede may not have lived to see freedom in his lifetime, but he packed a full life into the roughly four years he was active on the political scene. At his death he was emerging as a major figure in the ANC, and one wonders what his impact on the course of African politics would have been if he had lived longer. Would the Youth League have put his name forward as their candidate to succeed Dr. Xuma as ANC president in 1949? If he had become ANC president, would he have moderated his strong views on African nationalism or would he have kept African nationalist ideas in the forefront in the ANC? Could he have defused the dissension in the ANC and staved off the breakaway of the PAC in the late 1950s?

Lembede was an incandescent figure whose diverse talents and educational and professional accomplishments marked him for distinction. A self-made man, he overcame his humble origins and devoted his meagre resources and his considerable energy to complete three university degrees. A gifted linguist, he communicated with ease in seven languages. A lawyer, he was the first of his contemporaries to qualify to practice. A committed Christian, he sought to translate his beliefs into political action. A political philosopher, he crafted an ideology of liberation centered around the cornerstones of African unity and a spiritual Pan-Africanism. To his age-mates he was a standard-bearer for their aspirations. And his untimely passing was deeply mourned by his friends and opponents alike. After his death, some African school teachers went so far as to hang his picture in their classrooms to inspire their pupils.

Lembede's achievements as a politician were modest. Unseasoned politically when he moved to Johannesburg in 1943, he came under the tutelage of more experienced young politicians and he rapidly rose to leadership positions in the Youth League and the parent ANC. Impatient, zealous, and uncompromising, he was a ferocious combatant who led the Youth League charge to shake up an ANC reluctant to adopt militant tactics. These qualities were both an asset and a liability when it came to practical politics. On the one hand, he was prepared to take up causes, however formidable the odds; and he was not daunted by the prospect of taking on the power elites of both the white government and the ANC. On the other hand, his brashness and intolerance of other people's views could lead him into blind alleys such as his flirtation with fascism. Moreover, his attempts to pressure ANC leaders to boycott government bodies such as the NRC and expel Communists from the ANC executive were easily thwarted by the ANC's Old Guard.

Lembede's temperament was more suited to the barricades than the backroom. His strength was as a polemicist, not as a tactician. Thus it is his ideas which are his primary legacy. His advocacy of an exclusive African nationalism, that Africans had to emancipate themselves psychologically and rely on their own leadership in order to challenge white domination, and that national liberation took primacy over class struggle provoked heated debate, even within Youth League circles. But his ideas struck a popular chord with many; and they fuelled debates on race, class, and national identity that reverberate to this day.

Perhaps it is fitting to conclude this introduction by turning again to the words of Mda:

Anton Lembede became the most pronounced and the most forceful and uncompromising exponent of the new spirit. It is not that he was a prophet or a saint. There were other men around and behind him who were just as great. It is just that his language touched the inner chords in the hearts of the African people, and intensified the stirrings and the ferment which were already there. Anton Lembede spoke a language which reminded the people of their past greatness, and their present misery, and which opened up new boundless vistas of freedom and joy in a new democratic Africa. He gave "clear and pointed expression to the vaguely felt ideas of the age."[74]

ENDNOTES

1. The first serious scholarly assessment of Lembede is Gail Gerhart's *Black Power in South Africa* (Berkeley: University of California Press, 1978). See also A. J. G. M. Saunders, "Anton Muziwakhe Lembede — Pioneer of African Nationalism," *Codicillus,* XXVII, 2 (1986): 11–17.

2. Martin and Martha Lembede were married in 1912. Besides Muziwakhe, the Lembedes had four sons, Nicholas, Alpheus, Elias, and Victor and two daughters, Cathrene and Evelyn. This information on the Lembedes is largely drawn from a family history collected by Sister M. Edista Lembede, a daughter of Nicholas Lembede. We thank the Lembede family for sharing this history with us. We have also been helped by interviews with Phillipine Lembede, wife of Nicholas Lembede; Emeline, wife of Alpheus Lembede; Alpheus Makhanya, husband of Cathrene Lembede; and Anna Lembede, wife of Anton's father's brother, Michael. The interviews were held in Umbumbulu, 1 August 1992.

3. We do not know whether Martin Lembede was a labor tenant, a share-cropper, or a wage laborer on Frank Fell's farm. Detailed research on Umbumbulu has not been carried out, but an overview of farm evictions in Natal is found in Helen Bradford, *A Taste of Freedom: The ICU in Rural South Africa, 1924–1930* (New Haven: Yale University Press, 1987), chapter 2.

4. Letters from Sister Bernadette Sibeko to Robert Edgar; Interview with Sister Sibeko, Assisi Convent, Port Shepstone, August 1992.

5. We do not want to paint a one-dimensional portrait of a Lembede obsessed by his studies and work. His family and colleagues in the Youth League remember him as having a lively sense of humor.

6. Adams' founders, the American Board of Foreign Missions originally named the school Amanzimtoti Training Institute, but renamed it Adams College around 1914 after the American medical missionary Dr. Newton Adams, who had arrived in Natal in 1835. Before his death in 1851, Adams

founded a mission near what became the Training Institute. For a description of life at Adams, see Tim Couzens, *The New African: A Study of the Life and Work of H. I. E. Dhlomo* (Johannesburg: Ravan Press, 1985), 47–54. Dhlomo had been a student at Adams in the early 1920s. See also Edgar Brookes, *A South African Pilgrimage* (Johannesburg: Ravan, 1977), esp. chapters 4 and 5.

7. Jordan Ngubane, unpublished autobiography (Carter-Karis Collection).

8. Interview, Ellen Kuzwayo, August 1991.

9. Interview, Edna Bam, November 1984; Edwin Smith, *Aggrey of Africa: A Study in Black and White* (London: Student Christian Movement Press, 1929), 169–70.

10. Anton Lembede, "Language Study and the Bantu Student," *Iso Lomuzi,* IV, 2 (1935). Published annually from 1931 to 1956, *Iso Lomuzi* (Eye of the Villager) chronicled life at Adams College and especially featured student essays, poems and dramas.

A column, "Notes By the Way," in *Iso Lomuzi* (III, 2 (1934), 11), commented on Lembede's facility with languages: "Anton Lembede, a T3 student, has learnt to write Afrikaans practically without external assistance. This shows what can be done by a student who is determined to improve his education. His standard of English is also greatly above the average. He makes a careful note of any new words, phrases and idioms he meets with in these two languages. Our advice to those who are backward in the official languages of the Union is, 'Emulate Anton.'"

11. Lembede, "The Importance of Agriculture," *Iso Lomuzi,* IV, 1 (1934); "What Do We Understand by Economics," *Iso Lomuzi,* IV, 1 (1934).

12. Brookes, *A South African Pilgrimage,* 65. Brookes was Adams' principal from 1934 to 1945. A founding member of the Institute of Race Relations and its president from 1930 to 1932, Brookes had supported segregation in the 1920s but then shifted and became the archetypical white liberal. From 1937 to 1952 he was elected Senator representing Africans in Natal and Zululand in Parliament.

13. *Bantu World,* 17 November 1945. Praising African heroes was a two-sided coin. At the same meeting where Mnqoma spoke, Malcolm, the former Chief Inspector of Native Education in Natal, also lectured on the value of honoring heroes and ancestors.

14. Interview, Ellen Kuzwayo, August 1991.

15. According to Joe Matthews, Lembede planned to write a doctoral dissertation on the "Jurisprudential Basis of African Law," but we have no corroborative evidence for this.

16. *Ilanga lase Natal,* 29 September 1945.

17. Interview, B. M. Khaketla, Maseru, 14 May 1985.

18. Interview, Victor Khomari, Mafeteng, 1985.

19. A. M. Lembede to J. D. Rheinallt Jones, 16 June 1943, South African Institute of Race Relations Papers, AD843 RJ/Aa 11.7.7.

20. Seme was charged with neglecting the "interests" of some of his clients and for charging them "excessive, unreasonable and unconscionable fees." His career is treated in more detail in Craig Charney, "Pixley Seme '06: Father of the African National Congress," *Columbia College Today,* 14, 2 (Spring/Summer 1987): 15-17; Richard Rive and Tim Couzens, *Seme: The Founder of the ANC* (Johannesburg: Skotaville Publishers, 1991); and Christopher Saunders, "Pixley Seme: Towards A Biography," *South African Historical Journal* 25 (1991): 196-217.

21. Seme certainly understood that his status as a lawyer meant that Africans expected him to carry himself in a dignified manner. A contemporary of Lembede expressed his disapproval of another African lawyer of that era by relating how the lawyer would eat "fish and chips" and sit on the street-curbs with "ordinary" folk.

22. Native Affairs Commissioner, Johannesburg (KJB), Box 166, File 476/47, Central Archives, Pretoria. A successful businessman, Isaac Dhlomo (1911-1977) had started up a taxi and bus transport network between Durban and Umbumbulu in the 1930s. Besides helping Lembede, he was a benefactor of African causes, including Adams College and *Inkundla ya Bantu.* After he sold his businesses in the 1960s, he retired and was an active participant in educational issues, serving as the chairman of the Umbumbulu School Board. (We thank Oscar Dhlomo, one of Isaac's sons, for this information).

Lembede served his articles with Seme from January 1944 to January 1946 and qualified to practice as an attorney in February 1946. He qualified as a conveyancer in December 1946 after passing an exam. His qualification documents and conveyancer exam are found in the Transvaal Archives, Pretoria, in the files of the Transvaal Provincial Division (TPD) 137/1946, 506/1946, and 90/1947.

23. Interview, Ike Matlhare.

24. Interview, Godfrey Pitje (March 1995). Walter Sisulu confirmed that these kinds of incidents were common to Oliver Tambo and Nelson Mandela when they were practicing law.

25. Jordan Ngubane, unpublished autobiography (Carter-Karis Collection).

26. Gerhart, *Black Power,* 54.

27. Interview, A. P. Mda, July 1992. Even after A. P. married in early 1947, his wife Rose remembered many an occasion where Lembede dropped by their home for marathon discussions with A. P. that lasted through the

night. Rose would retire and wake up the following morning to find A. P. and Lembede, still fully clothed, asleep on a bed. (Interview, Rose Mda, January 1995.)

28. Gerhart, *Black Power,* 53.

29. There is a substantial literature on African protest during the Second World War and the origins of the Youth League. These works include: Gerhart, *Black Power*; Peter Walshe, *The Rise of African Nationalism in South Africa: the African National Congress, 1912-1952* (Berkeley: University of California Press, 1971); Tom Lodge, *Black Politics in South Africa Since 1945* (London: Longman, 1983); Thomas Karis, *From Protest to Challenge: A Documentary History of African Politics in South Africa* (Stanford: Hoover Institution Press, 1973), vol. 2; Baruch Hirson, *Yours for the Union: Class and Community Struggles in South Africa* (Johannesburg: Witwatersrand University Press, 1989); Miriam Basner, *Am I an African? The Political Memoirs of H. M. Basner* (Johannesburg: Witwatersrand University Press, 1993); Philip Bonner, "The Politics of Black Squatter Movements on the Rand, 1944-1952," *Radical History Review,* 46/7 (1990): 89-116; and Luli Callinicos, *A Place in the City: The Rand on the Eve of Apartheid* (Johannesburg: Ravan Press, 1993).

30. For a recent assessment of Xuma's presidency of the ANC, see Stephen Gish, "Alfred B. Xuma, 1893-1962: African, American, South African" (Ph.D. Dissertation, Stanford University, 1994), 169-230.

31. The most detailed account of the Youth League's founding is Karis and Carter, *From Protest to Challenge,* Vol. II, 98-106.

32. However, Moerane's participation in youth activities did not last long. When the ANC Youth League delegated Moerane to convene a Youth League in Natal, the Natal Department of Education sent him a letter warning him that, as a teacher, he could not engage in political activities. Faced with that choice, Moerane dropped out of Youth League activities (*Ilanga lase Natal,* 1 July 1944).

33. Tambo belonged to a group of six Fort Hare science students (most of them former students at St. Peter's School in Johannesburg) who styled themselves "The Syndicate" and who pledged themselves to work to better the world after their graduation. Besides Tambo, Congress Mbata, Joseph Mokoena, and Lancelot Gama participated in Youth League activities. (Interview, Lancelot Gama, October 1994.)

34. *Bantu World,* 8 January 1944.

35. *Bantu World,* 22 April 1944.

36. Jordan Ngubane, unpublished autobiography (Carter-Karis Collection).

37. Gwendolen Carter, interview with Congress Mbata, 19 February 1964, Carter-Karis Collection.

38. Minutes of ANC National Executive Meeting, February 1947, quoted in Thomas Karis and Gwendolen Carter, *From Protest to Challenge,* Vol. II, 266–72. Following Lembede's death, Youth Leaguers continued to press for a total boycott of the NRC. At the 1947 ANC conference Oliver Tambo's boycott resolution failed by 57 votes to 7. Eventually the government abolished the NRC in 1951 as it began constructing its apartheid structures.

39. *Inkululeko,* 9 September 1944.

40. Interview, Joe Matthews, August 1992. Matthews' account is supported by another St. Peter's alumnus, Nathaniel Masemola (Interview, July 1995).

Lembede's flair for the theatrical was evident on other occasions. Mda recalled a day when he and Lembede were going to address an afternoon meeting in Orlando. They arrived there early. Everyone else showed up late, so Lembede and Mda locked the doors, arranged the chairs, and started the meeting on their own. Lembede went ahead and harangued the empty chairs in front of him. By the time he had finished, people were clustered around the windows clamoring to be let in. The next time Lembede and Mda came for a meeting, the hall was packed before they arrived.

41. "Africanism," *T.A.S.A. Bulletin,* I, 2 (July 1944); Lembede, "National Unity Among Africans," *Ilanga lase Natal,* 6 October 1945; Lembede, "Policy of the Congress Youth League," *Inkundla ya Bantu,* May 1946; Lembede, "National Units," *Ilanga lase Natal,* 18 May 1946.

42. Lembede, "Some Basic Principles of African Nationalism," *Ilanga lase Natal,* 24 February 1945.

43. Lembede, "The Conception of God as Expounded by, or as it Emerges from the Writings of Philosophers from Descartes to the Present Day (M.A. Thesis, University of South Africa, 1945), 40.

44. Diederichs, quoted in Dunbar Moodie, *The Rise of Afrikanerdom: Power, Apartheid, and the Afrikaner Civil Religion* (Berkeley: University of California Press, 1975), 159.

45. Mary Benson Papers, University Research Library, University of California, Los Angeles.

46. Lembede, "African Nationalism and the New African Masses," *Ilanga lase Natal,* 21 June 1947; "Africanism," *T.A.S.A.Bulletin,* I, 2 (July 1944); "Know Thyself," *Bantu World,* 30 June 1945.

47. For an exposition of Blyden's ideas see Hollis Lynch, *Edward Wilmot Blyden Pan-Negro Patriot 1832-1912* (London: Oxford University Press, 1967). On the impact of Garvey's ideas on black South Africans see Robert Hill's introduction to a new edition of *The Philosophy and Opinions of Marcus Garvey* (New York: Atheneum, 1992), first published in 1923.

The Commentator (March-July 1968) quotes from a speech, "The Way Forward," Lembede supposedly delivered in 1943. Garvey is quoted in the speech, but we have been reluctant to reprint the speech because we are unsure about its authenticity or accuracy. Our reluctance is based on comparing a second Lembede speech, delivered just before his death and also reprinted in *The Commentator,* with the text of the same speech in the *African Advocate* (August/September 1947) (Document 22). The two speeches overlap in only a few places.

48. Lembede, "Policy of the Congress Youth League," *Inkundla ya Bantu,* May 1946.

49. *Inkululeko,* 23 September 1944. Lembede went on to add that rejecting white leadership of African organizations was not the same as repudiating all forms of white assistance.

50. "Last Message of Late Mr. A. M. Lembede, M.A., LL.B.," *African Advocate,* August/September 1947. Seme's fascination with Egypt and African history can be dated back to his years as a student at Columbia University in New York City. In 1906, he delivered a prize-winning speech, "The Regeneration of Africa," in which he boasted: "The pyramids of Egypt are structures to which the world presents nothing comparable. The mighty monuments seem to look with disdain on every work of human art and to vie with Nature herself. All the glory of Egypt belongs to Africa and her people. These monuments are the indestructible memorials of their great and original genius." (His speech is reprinted in Rive and Couzens, eds., *Seme,* 75-81 and Carter and Karis, *From Protest to Challenge,* Vol. I, 69-71.) We do not have evidence on where Seme's ideas on Egypt originated, but a likely source was the works of African-American historians of the time such as George Washington Williams who were championing the idea that Egypt was an African civilization. See Dickson Bruce, "Ancient Africa and the Early Black American Historians, 1883-1915," *American Quarterly,* XXXVI (1984): 684-699.

51. Lembede, "Book Review of B. Wallet Vilakazi's *Nje-Nempela,*" *Teachers' Quarterly Review,* I, 2 (1946), 81. The Bambatha rebellion spilled over into the Umbumbulu district, and Lembede probably heard stories by participants in the rebellion when he was growing up.

52. Lembede, "Fallacy of Non-European Unity Movement," *Bantu World,* 11 August 1945.

52. This argument appears in an article by Mda (using the pseudonym *"umAfrika"*). See "Anton Lembede — III," *The Africanist* (July/August 1955): 2-4.

53. Lembede, "African Trade Unions."

54. Lembede, "The I.C.U. and the A.N.C.," *Ilanga lase Natal,* 26 October 1946.

55. Lembede, "The Conception of God"; "African National Congress and Churches," *Umteteli wa Bantu,* 29 July 1945; "African Nationalism and the Christian Church," *Ilanga lase Natal,* 22 September 1945.

56. The full text of the resolution is contained in *Inkululeko,* 29 October 1945. Lembede hammered away at Communists, but he also had a practical side. David Bopape, a Communist as well as a Youth Leaguer, remembered Lembede attacking him for being a Communist; but as secretary of the Transvaal ANC, Bopape had no difficulty working with Lembede on political issues. (Interview, David Bopape, January 1995.)

57. After Lembede's death, Youth Leaguers unsuccessfully pressed the Transvaal ANC to pass a resolution prohibiting ANC officials from belonging to other political organizations. The resolution narrowly failed thirty-two to thirty (Peter Walshe, *The Rise of African Nationalism,* 357).

At least one prominent ANC figure cited pragmatic reasons for opposing the Youth League resolution. Roseberry Bokwe, a Middledrift medical doctor, was raising money from left-of-center American organizations, and he did not want a purge of the ANC left to jeopardize their support. (Interview, Joe Matthews, August 1992.)

58. "Letter from the ANC Youth League (Transvaal) to the Secretary of the Progressive Youth Council, 16 March 1945," in Thomas Karis and Gwendolen Carter, *From Protest to Challenge: A Documentary History of African Politics in South Africa, 1882–1964,* vol. 2, (Hoover Institution Press, 1973), 316.) The Youth League letter writer is not identified, but the tone and style are unmistakably Lembede's.

59. Lembede, "Some Basic Principles of African Nationalism," *Ilanga lase Natal,* 24 February 1945; "Policy of the Congress Youth League," *Inkundla ya Bantu,* May 1946.

60. His slogan, "after national freedom, then, socialism" had a vague resemblance to the two-stage approach of the Communist Party's Native Republic thesis, which had sparked off a divisive debate within the Party in the 1920s and 1930s and which was still being discussed in the 1940s. See Sadie Forman and Andre Odendaal, *A Trumpet From the Housetops: the Selected Writings of Lionel Forman* (Cape Town: David Philip, 1992), 83–87.

61. After Anton's death, the Buick conveyed Nicholas and his mother back to Umbumbulu and then was returned to Johannesburg and sold.

62. Lembede family history collected by Sister Edista Lembede.

63. Interviews, Lembede family, Umbumbulu, August 1992; Cherry Mndaweni, Ladysmith, January and July 1995. When Lembede died, Mndaweni came to Umbumbulu for a period of mourning during which a goat was slaughtered. She worked at Sibusiwe Makhanya's Umbumbulu clinic for a month before returning to her home.

64. Interview, Walter Sisulu, August 1992. Nelson Mandela and Lembede had served as best men at Walter's wedding. Walter remembered Lembede speaking at the wedding reception and telling his bride Albertina: "You have married a married man — he is married to the nation." (Interview, Walter Sisulu, March 1995.)

65. Several other explanations were offered for Lembede's sudden death. One rumor that circulated immediately after his death was that he was poisoned by a jilted girl friend. Another explanation was raised in a column by "SPQR"in *Inkundla ya Bantu* (5 November 1947) following the death of Dr. B. W. Vilakazi. The writer plaintively asked, "Why do we die so young?" and suggested the deaths of Lembede and Vilakazi may have been due to stress. They had pursued their studies and work so single-mindedly that they did not look after their physical well-being. "Anton Lembede used to boast that he never had set his foot in a tennis court. And those who knew him well will aver that no man cared so little about his food." (We thank Gail Gerhart for referring this article to us.)

66. Lembede family history collected by Sister Edista Lembede.

67. Lembede's grave site at Croesus cemetery is number 12226.

68. *Imvo Zabantsundu,* 3 August 1940.

69. A. P. Mda to Godfrey Pitje, 24 August 1948, ANC Collection (AD2186, LaIV), Witwatersrand University.

70. Karis and Carter, *From Protest to Challenge,* II, 328. Dennis Davis and Robert Fine have incorrectly interpreted this passage to mean that the Youth League had split into two camps — an extreme one espousing "racialism and radicalism" and a moderate one advocating "multi-racialism and liberalism." The problem with this reading is that Mda still remained faithful to African nationalism. The fissure in the Youth League only became apparent a few years later when Youth Leaguers like Sisulu, Tambo, and Mandela began straying from the nationalist position. (Dennis Davis with Robert Fine, *Beyond Apartheid: Labour and Liberation in South Africa* (Johannesburg: Ravan Press, 1991, 78).

71. See Mda's address at the 1955 Lembede Memorial Service in *The Africanist* (July/August 1955), 10.

72. *Bantu World,* 6 August 1955.

73. Interview, A. P. Mda, July 1992.

74. *umAfrika,* "Anton Lembede — III": 2-4.

EARLY
WRITINGS

I. A. M. LEMBEDE, "The Importance of Agriculture," *Iso Lomuzi*, Vol. IV, no. 1 (October 1934), 16-17.

AN INCENTIVE which has urged me to write this article is the tendency which is prevalent among my fellow-students and other people of underestimating the value of agriculture.

Agriculture is of primordial significance in the progress of a nation. No man can accurately trace the origin of agriculture because when man was created, God, the Great Agriculturalist had already planted a garden. So, the first work that was given by God to man was agricultural work.

Some educated people disparage manual labour; they say it is too inferior for them; they appreciate "white collar-work." Such people are rather destructive than constructive to a nation's progress. They do not do this because they have bottomless knowledge but because ignorance has got the upper hand of them.

A man may gain the highest university degrees and diplomas but he is not better than a well-trained and industrious farmer or carpenter. A leader in agriculture, carpentry, etc; is just as good as a leader in politics, science, education and arts.

Most of our people are not yet trained in agriculture, with the result that instead of preserving and using the soil properly, they aggravate the situation by reducing it to a useless state for agricultural activities. They always complain of the Government not giving them enough land for fields. But an Indian farmer gets rich and prosperous on one acre of land whereas an African farmer does not get this prosperity on ten or more acres of land. Why is that? This is the question for our intelligentsia to answer.

Town people with their industries, are dependent on farmers for supplies and for patronage. Failure of agriculture in a land can occasion incalculable catastrophe. Agriculture is the back-bone of a nation's life.

Therefore, I appeal to all African students who have an opportunity to enjoy agricultural lectures in institutions and other centres to apply the knowledge they have acquired after they leave school. The conception of despising manual labour should be deprecated. Remember how Booker T. Washington advocated manual training.[1] He was a leader indeed.

The damage done to the soil by our ignorant farmers, who are counted in millions, is inestimable. It not only brings misery, hunger, and poverty to them, but it also reduces the soil to a hopeless and helpless state for further occupation.

2. A. M. LEMBEDE, "What Do We Understand By Economics?", *Iso Lomuzi*, Vol. IV, no. 1 (October 1934), 20-21.

BY ECONOMICS we understand the science which investigates the manner in which nations or communities and their individual members get food, clothing, shelter, and whatever else is desirable or necessary for maintenance and improvement of the conditions of life, (such as the organisation of the community or nation — its history, customs, laws and many other factors which make life profitable.) Economic activities, therefore, consist in how the above-mentioned necessaries of life are dealt with.

WHAT DO WE UNDERSTAND BY RELIGION?

By religion, we understand such manifestations of feeling, thought and action in regard to God as are held to conduce to the welfare of the community or to that of individuals considered as members of the community. It is an obligation by which a man is bound to God. Religious activities, therefore, mean how the people try to procure this religious atmosphere. This country is predominated by the Christian religion; therefore I shall base my discussion on Christian principles and ideals. I need to mention here that economic activities are largely relevant to the material side of our lives whilst religious activities are largely relevant to the spiritual side.

ECONOMIC CONDITIONS IN BANTU RURAL COMMUNITIES:

Clothing is indecent where the primitive style of dressing obtains. Those who use European styles always imitate the Europeans in all unbecoming styles and thus waste money. Food is poor and unhygienic. Starvation always prevails.

Recreations are disregarded or unknown except singing. Natives are lazy and ignorant of working methods. Their methods of agriculture are absurdly awkward. Therefore, poverty is not uncommon. Laws of health are unknown or despised, and, as a result, the death rate is high. It should not surprise to hear that many rural Natives still regard education as something that is spoiling or demoralising. The ethical side of the community is always good on account of good laws. As for customs, some are good and others are bad or useless. Poverty which is brought about by the mentioned factors, drives many Natives from country to town.

HOW SHOULD I WORK TO HARMONIZE THE RELIGIOUS AND THE ECONOMIC ACTIVITIES?

Many Natives believe that in order to be a Christian, a man must wear gorgeous clothes. One day I asked one man who was simply and neatly dressed why he did not go to church. He answered that he had no good clothes. Therefore, to remedy this situation I would teach the people that Jesus does not want clothes but hearts of men. I would teach them to dress simply and neatly and thus save money from buying gorgeous clothes.

The man depends on food in order that he may achieve the work given to him by God on earth. The value of food does not depend on sweetness or taste but on the proteins and carbohydrates which the food contains. It is useless to buy costly kinds of food which have no food value. Therefore, I would instruct the people of the community to use the common kinds of food (which have proteins, carbohydrates, fats, vitamins) correctly; foods like milk, mealies, eggs and so forth.

Who can go to church or pray when he is sick? Recreations help to make us healthy and also save money which might have been spent on doctors. Is it not the aim of our Christian religion to create a good moral atmosphere and esprit de corps in communities? Recreations help to bring that about by making people come together and play together. They also thwart evil by making the people busy at their leisure time.

Our rural communities suffer greatly from poverty because Native people are lazy to work. They are also ignorant of working methods. Instead of using the soil they leave their communities and go to seek work among Europeans where they get very small wages. God says, "In the sweat of thy face shalt thou eat bread." He wants industrious people. He chose Gideon to lead the Israelites. He found him threshing corn. Elisha was called when he was ploughing; David was called when he was out with his father's flocks; Peter and Andrew were called when they were fishing, and so with many other cases. Therefore the people should be taught "the dignity of labour" and "how to labour." If one man can enable the community to be industrious one will be deserving the honour from all South Africans and from God.

Death stalks through the Natives' homes smiting down those they hold most dear. Booker T. Washington, realizing the importance of health, set aside some Sundays for health sermons instead of Gospel sermons. Why do not we do the same? Was it not the aim of Christ to heal? Therefore some Sundays or parts of Sundays should be set aside for lectures on laws of health. I would also visit the homes to see if the laws of health are applied, and give further demonstrations.

God intended us to develop to high perfection in our lives. The factor which helps us to reach that perfection is education. It is from educational sources that we have trains, aeroplanes, electricity, more appreciation of God's power, abolition of slavery, and many other things. Therefore, I would tell the people of the community about the importance of education and urge them to send their children to school. It will not be hard to send children to school if the people are industrious.

Such customs as Ilobolo[2] should be preserved because they are not against our religious principles. Ilobolo, for instance, confirms the marriage so that divorce is not easily possible. But, polygamy should be done away with, because in these days a man cannot afford to support many members of the family and the result will be distress and misery.

In order to impress these factors upon the minds of the people I would preach about them in chapels (where people come together). I would get texts from the Bible which bear upon these factors (as I have already quoted some). I would also visit homes of the people, and be an example of what I say. If my teachings can be carried out scrupulously I am sure the Native of to-morrow would differ from the Native of to-day and yesterday. His economical, ethical and political situation would change as a result of the HARMONIZATION OF ECONOMICAL AND RELIGIOUS ACTIVITIES.

Our communities are also menaced by liquor. In this case I would emphasize the harm that beer has on the body, and how it brings about poverty and many crimes. Although I would not be able to make the people abstain from beer totally I would influence them to drink moderately.

3. A. M. LEMBEDE, "Language Study And The Bantu Student," *Iso Lomuzi*, IV, no. 2 (June 1935), 9–10.

OF ALL the sciences, one I like best is Anthropology — the study of the antiquity of man and his development from savagedom to a high standard of civilisation. This science deals with many human institutions for example, growth of languages, religion, customs and so forth. I am particularly interested in the study of languages.

I write this article because students have approached me, asking how I manage to learn foreign languages so easily. I have been a student here for three years and in that period I have learnt four foreign languages — Afrikaans, Sesutho [sic], Xosa [sic] and now I am studying Latin.

The study of languages has a social value in that it helps one to live well with fellow-men who do not speak one's language. No man can deny that 50% of racial hatred in the world, arises because people speak different languages.

The economic value of studying languages is that a linguist can be employed where a non-linguist would not be employed.

Another value of language study is that the literature of the language studied is accessible.

The Bantu languages are still in their infancy, they are controlled by white people.[3] It speaks for itself, therefore, that we want educated Bantu men who have studied various Bantu languages, and who will be authorities on them.

As to the method of studying a new language, experts differ. Some say that a person should begin by reading the simplest reading book in that language in order to increase his vocabulary and then tackle Grammar; others say that a person should first tackle Grammar and then take up a simple reading book.

In my own experience of studying languages, however, I have found that the best way is to apply both methods at the same time. The periods of studying must be regular, at least thirty minutes a day. Speak the language as much as you can. Read as many books as you can written in the language studied.

If I get a Grammar book, a simple reading book and a dictionary, I can study any language, provided the medium of learning is a language I know. It is not easy, it is a struggle, but "nothing is given to mortals without toil."[4]

I am still anxious to learn five more languages — French, German, Shangaan, Sishona and Swahili.

4. A. M. LEMBEDE, "'n Noue Ontkoming [A Narrow Escape]," *Iso Lomuzi*, III, no. 1 (October 1933), 14.

ALMAL WAT in die noordelike deel van Natal woon, weet wat haël, reen, en donderstorms is.

Ons het naby Maritzburg in die buurte van Izingomankuluberg gewoon. Een dag — dit was 'n lieflike somermôre — was die hemel onbewolk en die son het opgekom met *sy* ['n] pragtige helder lig. My werk was om die beeste op te pas. Smôrens het ek hulle na die weiveld toe gedryf en saans weer huis-toe gebring.

Een agtermiddag voordat ek die beeste huis-toe gebring het, het wit wolke gevolg deur pikswartes aan die westelike horison te voorskyn gekom. Toe ek met die beeste by die huis kom was die hele hemel bewolk, en 'n mens kon die weerlig sien en die donder in die verte hoor. Dit het ook nie lank geduur nie voor die storm losgebars het. Die weerligte [weerlig] het geblits en die donderslae was gruwelik.

Ons kinders het nog buite op die werf gespeel, maar my vader het ons laat inkom om stil in die huis te bly. Geen vyf minute was verby nie of die storm tref ons huis. Daar die son reeds onder was, kon 'n mens niks buite sien nie behalwe as die weerlig alles vir 'n oomblik helder te voorskyn laat kom. Ons het van vrees gebewe, en ons kon sien dat my vader bekommerd was, want hy het op en af gestap. Ons huis, wat deur bome omring was, het op'n krans gestaan. So sterk was die wind dat die bome verbreek [gebreek] is.

Skielik het ek die huis se balk hoor kraak en toe stort die huis op ons in. Die dak is weggewaai en die mure het op ons geval. Hoe ek uitgekom het, weet ek nie. Ek vind my vader toe reeds besig om die ander onder die puin te probeer uitsleep. Ek het bitterlik gehuil, maar vader sê: "Moenie huil nie; alles sal regkom." Moeder en drie kinders was nog toe onder die omgevalle muur. Nog steeds het dit gedonder, gehaël en gereën, en baie bome het plat op die grond gelê.

Na tien minute het my vader daarin geslaag om my moeder en twee van die kinders uit te kry, maar my broertjie van ses jaar was nêrens te kry nie. Ons het gesoek en na hom geroep, maar tevergeefs. Na 'n lang ruk, egter, kry vader hom gelukkig, maar ons het gedink hy was dood. Tot ons vreugde vind ons hy is net bewusteloos. Spoedig het hy sy bewussyn terug gekry.

Dis 'n pikdonker nag. Ons huis lê in puin. Waarnatoe nou? Ons het aangesukkel na 'n kraal in die buurte. Dit het maar swaar gegaan, want my broertjie het 'n groot wond aan sy kop opgedoen, my moeder se been het seer gekry, en ek het my arm verstuit. Tog het ons eindelik ons bestemming bereik. Die storm was toe ook al verby en die mense het ons met die grootste vriendelikheid ontvang en ons bejammer; ook het hulle vir ons droë klere gegee aangesien ons s'n papnat was. By hulle, so hoor ons toe, het die weer drie beeste en vyf skape in die kraal doodgeslaan net voor ons aankoms.

Na die donderstorm verby was, het die wolke verdwyn, en die pragtige blou hemel met sy flikkerende sterre en helderskynende maan het te voorskyn gekom. Die skaduwees van die berge het te lieflik gelyk in die helder maanlig, terwyl paddas en kriekies hulle danklied laat hoor. Maar waar was ons huis?

Die volgende môre is ons na ons huis om te sien watter skade die storm aangerig het. Ons dag dat ons beeste almal nood [dood] was, maar hulle het daar heelhuids van afgekom. Hulle het gebulk van blydskap om ons te sien, en ek het hulle veld toe geja.

Elke aand nadat ek die beeste in die kraal by ons vernielde huis geja het, moes ek hulle laat staam [staan] en na die naburige kraal gaan. Hier is die liedjie, wat ek dan vir hulle sing:

O, beeste van my vader
Moenie treurig wees nie.
God het ons van julle geskei
Maar wat deur Hom gedoen is, is heeltemal goed.
Eendag sal ons weer bymekaar kom.
Moenie droewig wees nie.

Daarop het 'n bul met deurdringende gebulk geantwoord.

Ons het in daardie kraal vir tien dae gebly. My vader het 'n nuwe huis naby die oue gebou, en toe dit klaar was, kon ons weer naby ons beeste gaan woon. Die gewonde kind was toe al gesond, en ook ek en moeder is [het] herstel van ons kwetsure [kwetse]. Is dit nie 'n noue ontkoming waarvoor ons die Heer nooit genoeg dankbaar kan wees nie!

TRANSLATION

Everyone who lives in the northern part of Natal knows what hail, rain, and thunderstorms are.

We used to live near Maritzburg in the neighborhood of the Izingomankulu mountains. One day — it was a lovely summer day — the sky was clear and the sun was shining bright. My duty was to look after cattle. I drove them to the veld (grazing land) every morning and brought them home in the evening.

One afternoon, before I could bring the cattle home, I saw the white clouds followed closely by dark clouds on the western horizon. By the time I got home the whole sky was covered in clouds, and one could see the lightning and the thunder in the distance. It was not too long before the storm exploded. There was lightning and the thunder was roaring.

Some of us siblings were still playing outside in the yard but my father called us in and asked us to remain silent. Hardly five minutes had passed when the storm hit our house. The sun was completely covered by the clouds, one could see nothing except when the lightning struck and for a moment there was bright light. We were shaking with fear and we could see our father was worried because he kept pacing up and down. Our house, which was surrounded by trees was built on rocks. So strong was the wind, it broke these trees. Suddenly I heard the rafters of the house cracking and the house collapsed on us. The roof was blown away and the walls fell on us. How I got out, I still do not know. I found my father already busy trying to remove another one from the ruins. I cried bitterly but my father said, "Do not cry, everything will be fine." My mother and three other children were still trapped under the ruins. It still continued to thunder and to rain and many trees fell flat on the ground.

After about ten minutes my father succeeded in removing my mother and two of my siblings, but my six year old brother was nowhere to be found. We looked for him, called his name out aloud but to no avail. After a long time, actually, father luckily found him, but we were all thinking that he was dead. To our surprise, he had only lost consciousness. He quickly regained his consciousness.

It was a very dark night. Our house lay in ruins. Where to now? We all huddled in a homestead in the neighborhood. It was very difficult, because my brother had a big wound on his head, my mother had injuries on her leg and I had sprained my arm. At least we had reached our destination. The storm was over and the people received us with great warmth and friendliness and they took pity on us; they also gave us clean and dry clothes as ours were wet. We also heard from them that the storm killed three cattle and five sheep from one village before our arrival.

After the storm had passed, the clouds cleared and the beautiful blue sky was filled with twinkling stars, a full moon came into view. The shadows of the mountain looked beautiful against the moonlight, while the frogs and crickets croaked their thankful prayers. But, where was our house?

The following morning, we went to our house to see what damage the storm had inflicted on us. We thought that all our cattle were dead but they had emerged unscathed by this whole experience. They bellowed and mooed from excitement when they saw us, and I drove them to the veld.

Every night after putting the cattle away in the kraal near our destroyed house, I would have to leave them and go to the nearby kraal where we were accommodated. Here is a poem, that I would recite for them:

Oh, cattle of my father
Please do not be sad.
God has separated us from you.
But what has been done by Him.
Is absolutely correct.
One day we shall come together.
Please do not be sad.

Thereafter a bull would bellow with a piercing moo as if in reply.

We stayed at the new kraal for ten days. Father built a new house near the old one, and when it was finished we could live closer to our cattle again. The most wonderful thing was that we recovered from our injuries. Was this not a narrow escape for which we will always be grateful to God!

5. A. M. LEMBEDE, "Trees and Their Value to Human Beings," *Native Teachers' Journal*, XVIII, no. 3 (April 1939), 119–120.

ON EMBARKING upon a subject of such importance one needs to be more highly qualified than I am in order that it may receive its due stress.

Trees provide food for human beings, as well as shade and shelter for animals and birds. They are also of great economic importance in supplying timber for building and furniture and in modern times for woodpulp from which paper is made.

It is not, however, from the material standpoint but from their decorative effect, which provides beautiful scenery and breaks the monotony of barren stretches of land, that we want to consider trees. There is a good deal more that could be said about the importance of trees, but for my purpose it is unnecessary to probe any deeper for mere geographical purposes.

When we walk about among beautiful trees with flowers perfuming the sky, we realise that it is our duty to acknowledge with thanks the inheritance bequeathed to us by Nature.

We, as teachers and Agricultural demonstrators, should explain to our Native people the necessity for trees on their lands and at their homes, and thus prevent their indiscriminate destruction.

Let us encourage children to plant trees. During fruit time boys steal a great deal. They even rob the European farmers of their fruit. The habit of theft in this way develops and this is one of many unheeded tendencies which spoil the morals of our children. If they had plenty of fruit at their homes they would have no desire to steal.

One feels ashamed to come across a teacher's cottage without a single tree or flower, or with some poor specimens of fruit trees, inferior in type and variety.

My fellow teachers let us prove ourselves as true leaders of our nation by our example. We should have our homes surrounded with varieties of fruit trees of a standard type. Flowers and ornamental trees should beautify our homes.

Firstly by our example and then by precept we can improve the present conditions prevailing amongst Natives, of considering trees as something to be hewn down for fire wood, and the lack of appreciation of fruit trees as assets to the homes, should be our concern.

Unless we are able to exemplify in a practical way the benefits derived from education, our illiterate brothers and sisters and the rank and file, will easily talk us out and we shall ever confirm our diminished prestige as at present.

(submitted from Maria Ratschitz Mission, P.O. Waschbank)

CONGRESS
YOUTH
LEAGUE
ACTIVITIES

6. "CONGRESS YOUTH LEAGUE MANIFESTO," Issued by the Provisional Committee of the Congress Youth League, March 1944.

PREAMBLE

WHEREAS Africanism must be promoted i.e. Africans must struggle for development, progress and national liberation so as to occupy their rightful and honourable place among nations of the world;

AND WHEREAS African Youth must be united, consolidated, trained and disciplined because from their ranks future leaders will be recruited;

AND WHEREAS a resolution was passed by the conference of the African National Congress held in Bloemfontein in 1943, authorising the founding and establishment of the Congress Youth League,

WE therefore assume the responsibility of laying the foundations of the said Youth League.

STATEMENT OF POLICY

South Africa has a complex problem. Stated briefly it is: The contact of the White race with the Black has resulted in the emergence of a set of conflicting living conditions and outlooks on life which seriously hamper South Africa's progress to nationhood.

The White race, possessing superior military strength and at present having superior organising skill has arrogated to itself the ownership of the land and invested itself with authority and the right to regard South Africa as a Whiteman's country. This has meant that the African, who owned the land before the advent of the Whites, has been deprived of all security which may guarantee him an independent pursuit of destiny or ensure his leading a free and unhampered life. He had been defeated in the field of battle but refuses to accept this as meaning that he must be oppressed, just to enable the Whiteman to further dominate him.

The African regards Civilisation as the common heritage of all Mankind and claims as full a right to make his contribution to its advancement and to live free as any White South African; further, he claims the right to all sources and agencies to enjoy rights and fulfill duties which will place him on a footing of equality with every other South African racial group.

The majority of Whitemen regard it as the destiny of the White race to dominate the man of colour. The harshness of their domination, however, is rousing in the African feelings of hatred of everything that bars his way to full and free citizenship and these feelings can no longer be suppressed.

In South Africa, the conflict has emerged as one of race on the one side and one of ideals on the other. The whiteman regards the Universe as a gigantic machine hurtling through time and space to its final destination; individuals in it are but tiny organisms with private lives that lead to private deaths; personal power, success and fame are the absolute measures of values; the things to live for. This outlook on life divides the Universe into a host of individual little entities which cannot help being in constant conflict thereby hastening the approach of the hour of their final destruction.

The African, on his side, regards the Universe as one composite whole; as an organic entity, progressively driving towards greater harmony and unity whose individual parts exist merely as interdependent aspects of one while realising their fullest life in the corporate life where communal contentment is the absolute measure of values. His philosophy of life strives towards unity and aggregation; towards greater social responsibility.

These divergences are not simplified by the fact that the two major races are on two different planes of achievement in the Civilisation of the West. This is taken advantage of to "civilise" the African with a view to making him a perpetual minor. This obstruction of his progress is disguised as letting him "develop along his own lines." He is, however, suspicious of any "lines" of development imposed on him from above and elects to develop along what the Natives Representative Council recently called the "lines of his own choosing."[5]

In practice these divergences and conflicts work to the disadvantage of the African. South Africa's 2,000,000 Whites are highly organised and are bound together by firm ties. They view South African problems through the perspective of Race destiny; that is the belief that the White race is the destined ruler and leader of the world for all time. This has made it imperative for the African to view his problems and those of his country through the perspective of Race. Viewing problems from the angle of Race destiny, the Whiteman acts as one group in relations between Black and White. Small minorities view South African problems through the perspective of Human destiny. These number among their ranks the few Whites who value Man as Man and as above Colour. Yet these are so few that their influence on national politics is but little felt.

The advantages on the side of the Whites enable 2,000,000 Whitemen to control and dominate with ease 8,000,000 Africans and to own 83% of the land while the Africans scrape a meagre existence on the remaining 17%. The Whiteman means to hold on to these gains at all costs and to consolidate his position, has segregated the African in the State, the Church, in Industry, Commerce etc., in all these relegating him to an inferior position where it is believed, the African will never menace White domination.

TRUSTEESHIP

To mislead the world and make it believe that the Whiteman in South Africa is helping the African on the road to civilised life, the Whiteman has arrogated to himself the title and role of Trustee for the African people.

The effects of Trusteeship alone have made the African realise that Trusteeship has meant, as it still means, the consolidation by the Whiteman of his position at the expense of the African people, so that by the time national awakening opens the eyes of the African people to the bluff they live under, White domination should be secure and unassailable.

A hurried glance at legislation passed by the Trustees for the African during the last forty years shows what a bluff Trusteeship is. The very Act of Union itself established as a legal right the claim of the Whiteman to dominate the man of colour.[6] It did not recognise the African as a citizen of the then newly-formed Union; it regarded him as a beggar at the gate.

This was followed by the 1913 Land Act[7] which deprived the African of Land and Land Security and in that way incapacitated him for that assertion of his will to be free which might otherwise have been inspired by assured security and fixed tenure. The Act drove him into urban areas where he soon made his way into skilled trades etc. But the Trustees had not brought him to urban areas to civilise him by opening to him avenues to skilled work. They had brought him so that he might be a cheap and nearby reserve of unskilled labour. This was finally established by the Colour Bar Act which shut Africans from skilled trades etc., thereby blocked their way to Civilisation via these channels.[8]

In 1923 the Trustees passed the Urban Areas Act and this measure as amended warned Africans clearly that they were bidding farewell to freedom.[9]

This Act imposed forms of control on the Africans which would have stirred into revolt any other section of the population. But because the Africans were not organised they yielded to more oppression and allowed themselves to be "controlled" from birth to the grave. This control had the effect of forcing Africans to remain impotent under unhealthy urban conditions which were set up to add their due to the ruining of the African's resistance to disease. The legalized slums, politely called Native Locations, were one aspect of these conditions.

But the Trustees were not satisfied with the emasculation of an entire community. In the 1927 Native Administration Act, they established the White race as the Supreme Chief of the African people. The conquest of the African people was complete.[10]

As the African accepted none of these measures to "civilise" him without a struggle, the Trustees had always been worried by his prospects as long as the Cape Franchise remained.[11] With little compunction, in 1936 the last door to citizenship was slammed in the face of the African by the Natives Representation Act which gave us 3 Whitemen to represent 8,000,000 Africans in a house of 150 representing 2,000,000 Whites.[12] At the same time a Land Act was passed to ensure that if the 1913 Land Act had left any openings for the African, then the Natives Land and Trust Act would seal them in the name of "humanity and Modern civilisation."[13]

The 1937 Native Laws Amendment Act closed up any other loophole through which the African could have forced his way to full citizenship.[14] Today, Trusteeship has made every African a criminal still out of prison. For all this we had to thank the philosophy of Trusteeship.

While Trustees have been very vocal in the solicitations for the African their deeds have shown clearly that talk of Trusteeship is an eyewash for the Civilised world and an empty platitude to soothe Africans into believing that after all oppression is a pleasant experience under Christian democratic rule. Trusteeship mentality is doing one thing and that very successfully, to drive the African steadily to extermination. Low wages, bad housing, inadequate health facilities, "Native education," mass exploitation, unfixed security on land and halfhearted measures to improve the African's living conditions are all instruments and tools with which the path to African extermination is being paved.

But the African rejects the theory that because he is non-White and because he is a conquered race, he must be exterminated. He demands the right to be a free citizen in the South African democracy; the right to an unhampered pursuit of his national destiny and the freedom to make his legitimate contribution to human advancement.

For the last two hundred years he has striven to adapt himself to changing conditions and has made every exertion to discover and derive the maximum benefits from the claims of the Whiteman that they are his Trustees. Instead of meeting with encouragement commensurate with his eagerness and goodwill he has been saddled with a load of oppression dating from the unprovoked wars of the last century and now containing such choice discriminating legislation as the 1913 Land Act and such benefits of Trusteeship as official harshness which recently attempted to hand an African under the very roof of the very State Department established to protect him and guide him on his way to civilisation just because he could not answer questions as quickly as the impatience of the Pass Office Trustees wanted.

In this very war South Africa is fighting against oppression and for Freedom; a war in which she has committed herself to the principle of freedom for all. In spite of this however it would be the highest folly to believe that after the war South Africa will treat the Africans as a citizen with the right to live free. South African blood . . . of Whites and Africans alike . . . has been shed to free the White peoples of Europe while Africans within the Union remain in bondage.

For his loyalty to the cause of human freedom and for his sacrifices in life, cash and kind, he has been promised a "Suspense Account" . . . another way of telling him that in spite of all he has done for his country in its hour of darkest need, for him there will be no freedom from fear and want.

LOSS OF FAITH IN TRUSTEESHIP

These conditions have made the African lose all faith in all talk of Trusteeship. HE NOW ELECTS TO DETERMINE HIS FUTURE BY HIS OWN EFFORTS. He has realised that to trust to the mere good grace of the Whiteman will not free him as no nation can free an oppressed group other than that group itself.

Self-determination is the philosophy of life which will save him from the disaster he clearly sees on his way . . . disasters to which Discrimination, Segregation, Pass Laws and Trusteeship are all ruthlessly and inevitably driving him.

The African is aware of the magnitude of the task before him but has learnt that promises no matter from what high source, are merely palliatives intended to drug him into yielding to more oppression. He has made up his mind to sweat for his freedom; determine his destiny himself and, THROUGH HIS AFRICAN NATIONAL CONGRESS IS BUILDING A STRONG NATIONAL UNITY FRONT WHICH WILL BE HIS SUREST GUARANTEE OF VICTORY OVER OPPRESSION.

THE AFRICAN NATIONAL CONGRESS

The African National Congress is the symbol and embodiment of the African's will to present a united national front against all forms of oppression, but this has not enabled the movement to advance the national cause in a manner demanded by prevailing conditions. And this, in turn, has drawn on it criticisms in recent times which cannot be ignored if Congress is to fulfill its mission in Africa.

The critics of Congress attribute the inability of Congress in the last twenty years to advance the national cause in a manner commensurate with the demands of the times, to weaknesses in its organisation and constitution, to its erratic policy of yielding to oppression, regarding itself as a body of gentlemen with clean hands and to failing to see the problem of the African through the proper perspective.

Those critics further allege that in that period Congress declined and became an organisation of the privileged few . . . some Professionals, Small Traders, a sprinkling of Intellectuals and Conservatives of all grades. This, it is said, imparted to the Congress character traits of reactionism and conservatism which made Congress a movement out of actual touch with the needs of the rank and file of our people.

It is further contended by the critics of Congress that the privileged few who constituted the most vocal elements in Congress that they strongly resented any curtailment of what they considered their rights and, since the popularisation of the Congress character would have jeopardised or brought about the withdrawal of those rights by the Authorities, Congress was forced to play the dual role of being unconscious police to check the assertion of the popular will on the one hand and, on the other, of constantly warning the authorities that further curtailment of the privileges of the few would compel them, the privileged few, to yield to pressure from the avalanche of popular opinion which was tired of appeasing the Authorities while life became more intolerable.

These privileged few, so the critics of Congress maintain, are not an efficiently organised Bloc. Their thinking itself lacks the national bias and this has made Congress a loose association of people who merely react negatively to given conditions, able neither to assert the national will nor to resist it openly. In this connection, Congress is accused of being partly suspicious of progressive thought and action, though it is itself unable to express correctly the views of the mass of the people.

Finally, the critics say that because the privileged few who direct Congress are poorly organised and have no marked following, Congress cannot openly defy popular wishes; hence to maintain its precarious existence, it is compelled to be very vocal against legislation that has harsh effects on the African underdog while it gives no positive lead nor has any constructive programme to enforce the repeal of all oppressive legislation.

CHALLENGE TO YOUTH

Some of these criticisms are founded on fact, it is true, but it does not advance the national cause if people concentrate on these while little or no effort is made to build Congress from within. It is admitted that in the process of our political development, our leadership made certain blunders. It was inevitable that this should have been the case, encompassed as the African people were and still are with forces inimical to their progress. But it does no good to stop at being noisy in condemning African leaders who went before us. Defects in the organisation of the people against oppression cannot be cured by mouthing criticisms and not putting our heads together to build what has been damaged and to find a way out of the present suffering.

Both the oppression and the causes that give rise to the criticisms of Congress cannot be allowed to go on indefinitely. Soon the point must be reached when African Youth, which has lived through oppression from the cradle to the present, calls a halt to it all. That point, happily is now reached . . . as witness some of the clear-cut national demands by Youth at the Bloemfontein conference and the formation of Youth movements and political parties.[15] All this is proof that youth wants action and is in sympathy with the rank and file of our oppressed people. It is all a challenge to Youth to join in force in the national fight against oppression.

In response to the demands of the times African Youth is LAYING ITS SERVICES AT THE DISPOSAL OF THE NATIONAL LIBERATION MOVEMENT, THE AFRICAN NATIONAL CONGRESS, IN THE FIRM BELIEF, KNOWLEDGE AND CONVICTION THAT THE CAUSE OF AFRICA MUST AND WILL TRIUMPH.

CONGRESS YOUTH LEAGUE

The formation of the African National Congress Youth League is an answer and assurance to the critics of the national movement that African Youth will not allow the struggles and sacrifices of their fathers to have been in vain. Our fathers fought so that we, better equipped when our time came, should start and continue from there they stopped.

The formation of this League is an attempt on the part of Youth to impart to Congress a truly national character. It is also a protest against the lack of discipline and the absence of a clearly-defined goal in the movement as a whole.

The Congress Youth League must be the brains-trust and power-station of the spirit of African nationalism; the spirit of African self-determination; the spirit that is so discernible in the thinking of our Youth. It must be an organisation where young African men and women will meet and exchange ideas in an atmosphere pervaded by a common hatred of oppression.

At this power-station the League will be a co-ordinating agency for all youthful forces employed in rousing popular political consciousness and fighting oppression and reaction. It will educate the people politically by concentrating its energies on the African homefront to make all sections of our people Congress-minded and nation-conscious.

But the Congress Youth League must not be allowed to detract Youth's attention from the organisation of Congress. In this regard, it is the first step to ensure that African Youth has direct connections with the leadership of Congress.

Circumstances call upon African Youth to make the League specialize in championing the cause of Africa; and to serve this end best, the League will sponsor a Congress political bloc, the Congress Progressive Group within the national movement. This will be the wing of the Youth League entrusted with the duty of organising Youth with a view to enabling it to make it accept the view that young people may organise and express better their political wishes outside of Congress; hence the formation of the bloc within Congress.

The Congress Progressive Group will stand for certain clear-cut national ideals within Congress; it will stand for specialisation within the national movement, to reinforce the latter's representative character and to consolidate the national unity front; it will keep a vigilant eye on all un-national tendencies on the national unity front and in Congress policies.

We must be honest enough to realise that neither Congress nor the African people can make progress as one amorphous mass. At a certain state we must cultivate specialised political attitudes. Failure to recognise this will wreck Congress and encourage revolts from it until it ceases to be a force in national politics.

By recognising this fact, Youth does not confess sympathy with those who revolted against the national movement.[16] These failed to realise that the formation of parties out of Congress was a serious weakening of the national unity front. They recognised the fact that

Congress is a national liberation movement but were not sufficiently experienced politically to form their party within the national fold and to develop opposition from within, while strengthening the national unity front.

The result of their inexperience has been the creation of serious rifts and splits on the national unity front. For this, there can be no pardon because we cannot afford to cause any rift on the national unity front at this critical moment. By weakening the national unity front we invite more oppression for Africans after the war. By strengthening the national unity front, we are preparing a strong front against onslaughts that will be made on their real aims of the national struggle and on its significance and makes the co-ordination of our political activities difficult, with the result that the African cannot take advantage of situations which, if intelligently exploited on time, may bring the African nearer full and free citizenship.

Congress is destined for a great purpose and mission, but short-sighted policies will cripple and make it unable to rise to its destiny. To prevent this and therefore the setting back of the clock of African progress, African Youth must join the League in their numbers to strengthen the national movement in view of the fact that divisions just now are being sown among the people by sections of the so-called privileged few, while no convincing effort is made to narrow down and finally eliminate the gulfs that divide our people even by those who clamour loudest for national unity. Those who sow these divisions direct their activities against the national unity front in order to make the national movement incapable of expressing the wishes of the people effectively; they are the enemies of a free Africa.

The Congress is the symbol of the African people's common hatred of all oppression and of their Will to fight it relentlessly as one compact group. Youth recognises the existence of specialised attitudes and where these lead to differences of opinion, that must be strictly a domestic matter within the national liberation movement and must in no way be allowed to interfere with the national unity front.

THE IDEAL OF NATIONAL UNITY MUST BE THE GUIDING IDEAL OF EVERY YOUNG AFRICAN'S LIFE

OUR CREED

a.) We believe in the divine destiny of nations.
b.) The goal of all our struggles is Africanism and our motto is "AFRICA'S CAUSE MUST TRIUMPH."
c.) We believe that the national liberation of Africans will be achieved by Africans themselves. We reject foreign leadership of Africa.
d.) We may borrow useful ideologies from foreign ideologies, but we reject the wholesale importation of foreign ideologies into Africa.
e.) We believe that leadership must be the personification and symbol of popular aspirations and ideals.
f.) We believe that practical leadership must be given to capable men, whatever their status in society.
g.) We believe in the scientific approach to all African problems.
h.) We combat moral disintegration among Africans by maintaining and upholding high ethical standards ourselves.
i.) We believe in the unity of all Africans from the Mediterranean Sea in the North to the Indian and Atlantic Oceans in the South . . . and that Africans must speak with one voice.

OUR PROGRAMME . . . . . THE THREE-YEAR PLAN

a.) Drafting and framing of the Constitution.
b.) Improving and consolidating our financial position.
c.) Establishing the Congress Progressive Group.
d.) To win over and persuade other Youth Organisations to come over to the African National Congress Youth League, i.e. to create national unity and consolidate the national unity front.
e.) To win over and persuade other African Organisations to come over to and pool their resources in the African National Congress, i.e. to create national unity and consolidate the national unity front.
f.) To make a critical study of all those forces working for or against African progress.

7. A. L. LEMBEDE, "The Congress Youth League: Its Attitude to Other Bantu Youth Organisations," *Bantu World,* 27 May 1944 (also printed in *Umteteli wa Bantu,* 27 May 1944 and *Inkundla ya Bantu,* 31 May 1944).

THE PRESENT century has been well called the century of youth. All over the world youth is in revolt against barren conservatism, stagnation and retrogression in society. Eminent leaders of mankind are beginning to realise more and more that a leader who has the youth behind him has the future in his hands.

"Man is a political animal," said Aristotle.[17] Yes, the political position of the Africans today is disfigured by disorder, chaos and pandemonium. Petty feuds and personal vendettas, divisions, dissensions, rifts, sects and schisms are the order of the day. Such a state of affairs is intolerable. Divisions weaken the nation and render it impotent and helpless.

There are some little and contemptible men who pride themselves on being leaders and who delight in these divisions and do all they can to fan the embers of these dissensions.

Youth is out to smash all political and other divisions. Those quasi-leaders who encourage divisions will be purged. Such leaders will be ostracized because they are traitors and quislings; they are betraying the national cause so they must be destroyed. Youth is now determined to create system out of disorder, cosmos out of chaos, and order out of the pandemonium.

We have now reached a critical stage in our national and political development a stage which can be epitomised by the cry "Unite or Perish!" We can only be saved by following and acting according to an ancient adage: ex unitate vires (Out of unity comes strength).

It was the realisation of some of the problems of the critical stage which led the African National Congress to adopt a resolution that a Congress Youth League be founded in order to strengthen and reinforce the A.N.C. in its national struggle. There are several other African Youth organisations in the country, e.g. Mr. Mnguni's Youth League in Johannesburg.[18]

The Congress Youth League is not necessarily hostile to these youth organisations, but earnestly seeks harmonious co-operation with them. The question which the Congress Youth League puts to these organisations is "Are you working for the national cause?" If the answer is "yes" then the Congress Youth League exhorts to the famous words of Mr. Churchill, "Let us go forward together."

8. ANTON LEMBEDE, "Congress Youth League and Future Plans," *Umteteli wa Bantu,* 24 June 1944.

LARGE-SCALE preparations have been initiated for the convocation of a Youth conference or rally in the Transvaal under the auspices of the Congress Youth League. At this Conference the rules and regulations of the League will be submitted for approval, members will be formally enrolled, a permanent executive committee of the League will be elected, and plans for future action will be drawn up. The provisional committee of the Youth League thus appeals to and invites all African young men and women of the Transvaal to get ready for this great conference. Whether you are a teacher or student, whether you are a graduate or illiterate, whether you are working in kitchen or factory, whether you are a street sweeper or gardener — COME!

The Transvaal section of the Congress youth wishes to congratulate the youth leaders of Natal who have founded a section of the Congress Youth League in Natal. We look forward to a day when the Youth League of Natal and that of the Transvaal and other provinces will meet at a round-table conference to coordinate plans and programmes of action, for "We are drawing up plans and laying foundations for a longer future than we can imagine."

Mr. C. S. Ramohanoe,[19] the newly elected president of the A.N.C. (Transvaal), a leader who is at home both with the masses and with the intellectuals, has requested the Transvaal Congress Youth League to provide him with speakers who will accompany him and appear with him on the platform at the Congress meetings which he is addressing on the Reef and Pretoria. He wants these speakers to help him in preaching Congress and Congress Youth League to the masses.

The Youth League cordially appreciates Mr. Ramohanoe's attitude and constructive policy.

To-day people are joining the Congress. All over the country the cry is: "Back to the Congress — our Mother organisation." The African National Congress is determinedly marching on. Mayibuye i Africa, Maluphakanyisa uphondo lwa yo, Morena boloka sechaba sa heso, ufolise lintoa le matsoenyeho. [Come back Africa, Let her horn be lifted, God protect our nation, He puts an end to wars and suffering.] We now expect the Congress Youth League to be established in the O.F.S., Cape, Protectorates, South-West Africa, Portuguese East Africa and Rhodesia. It is imperatively necessary, because African youth must take part in the titanic struggle for African nationalism and contribute substantially to the creation of the New African Order.

9. "AFRICAN YOUTH PLANS FOR THE FUTURE," *Inkundla ya Bantu,* December First Fortnight, 1945.

THE TRANSVAAL section of the Congress Youth League recently met in conference and among its high spots was Mr. A. M. Lembede's Presidential address, extracts from which we publish below. Mr. Lembede started by outlining the history and achievements of the Congress Youth League and then continued:

From the above, it is plain and evident that the Youth League cannot boast of glorious achievements so far. Its achievements indeed are a negligible small fraction of the vast and colossal task that still lies ahead. There has been no intensive campaign to found branches though rudimentary branches have been established at Pretoria, Wilberforce, Alexandra Township, Orlando, Springs etc. etc.

The periodic stages of the growth and development of the Youth League can be marked out as follows:

1944 was the year of establishment of the Youth League; 1945 was the year of its consolidation; 1946 will be the year of its militant expansion. We are aware of the vast tasks which still lie ahead for we are drawing plans and laying foundations for a longer future than we can imagine.

The approach of our Youth League to the burning problems and hardships confronting African youth purports to be scientific. Hence the League must tackle practical problems and daily issues facing African youth such as providing and popularising games and sports of all descriptions; striving for free and compulsory education and for more and better schools; launching a mass literacy campaign by establishing and assisting night schools; promoting and defending the interests of juvenile workers in Factories, Kitchens and everywhere; and combating juvenile delinquency in all its sinister forms and manifestations and by providing ethical values and ideals that will elevate and improve the moral tone of the youth. The League aims at balanced national progress — politically, economically, socially, educationally, culturally and ethically.

Other Provinces

Our Youth League is the National Youth League; that is why it was the President-General himself who gave the League the inaugural benediction. A National Youth League conference of all provinces was convened at Kimberley in December last year. The attendance was small so those present decided that no new election would take place but that the present executive continues [to] organise the League in the Transvaal as well as in the other provinces including the Protectorates. As soon as we have a fair number of branches in the Transvaal, a provincial conference shall be convened in order to elect the provincial President and Executive. The other provinces will be organised by the employment of such methods as the appointment of local organisers or organising committees.

Other Youth Leagues

As far as other African Youth Leagues and Organisations are concerned, our primary task is to win them over and integrate them in our League. But where it is impractical we advocate a policy of co-operation on common issues whenever possible.

Some time during this year, our League was invited to affiliate to the Progressive Youth Council with its South African Headquarters

in Johannesburg. Our Executive felt that our League could not affiliate to the Progressive Youth Council for the following reasons, *inter
alia:*

a.) Our Youth League is sovereign in Africa and over African
Youth: hence it cannot be a subordinate part of any other
youth organisation in Africa.

b.) Ours, being a Congress Youth League, the prior approval of
the A.N.C. was necessary before such an affiliation could be
considered on its merits.

The End of War and the Post War Problems

World War No. 2 has come to an end after a most barbaric human
slaughter in the history of our planet. Many Africans hoped that the
end of war the way it ended, would open up a vista of a new political
and economic order in South Africa, that it would lead to the ameliora-
tion rather than the deterioration of the position of the African in the
body politic of South Africa. But such credulous people are standing
aghast disillusioned and disenchanted today.

It is a rude awakening to such native people to observe that freedom
for the African people is out of sight, that economic exploitation and
political oppression of the African masses are being grimly intensified.
As usual, it is youth that has to suffer most; take for instance, the Pass
Laws section seventeen and the danger of the proposed transfer of the
administration of passes from the Native Affairs Department to the
Municipalities.

Organised African youth must fight this satanic system with all
powers at its disposal. Think again of the proposed youth labour
camps which mean slave labour, forced labour.

The Future

In conclusion may I don the cloak of a prophet and essay to predict
the future of the Congress Youth League. The future is a closed book
for us. What we know is we have so far achieved practically nothing
and that momentous tasks of vast dimensions and stupendous pro-

portions still await us in the future. We are not called to peace, com-
fort and enjoyment, but to hard work, struggle and sweat. We need
young men and women of high moral stamina and integrity; of courage and vision. In short, we need warriors. This means that we have
to develop a new type of youth — not the pleasure-loving, frivolous,
dissolute, light minded type — but youth of stoical discipline, trained
to endure suffering and difficulties. It is only this type of youth that
will achieve the national liberation of the African people. As Spinoza
says, we must look at whatever we do "Sub specie aeternitatis" —
under a form of eternity.

Although the outlook is so gloomy yet we unfalteringly hope that
ultimately we shall surmount even the apparently insuperable hardships and difficulties. Hope is our driving and unfailing force; for, as
the poet says: "Hope springs eternal in the human breast. Man never
is but always to be blest."[20]

10. A. M. LEMBEDE, "The Congress Youth League," *Bantu World,*
18 January 1947.

THE DECISION of the African National Congress about three
years ago, to form a youth league under Congress, was a very progressive step indeed. It is imperatively necessary to mobilise the nation in
all its ramifications — men, women and young people. It is specially
necessary that young people be imbued and indoctrinated with Congress spirit based on African nationalism — the ideology underlying
our struggle for national liberation. It is an incontrovertible and un-
challengeable fact that the leaders of to-morrow will be recruited
from the youth of to-day. No man outside the lunatic asylum can
shamelessly maintain that present leaders are immortal. They must,
when the hour strikes, inexorably bow down to fate and pass away,
for: "There is no armour against fate, Death lays his icy hand on
Kings."[21]

Political parties and organisations in most countries spend huge
sums of money and much energy in organising and mobilising youth.
The organisation of the A.N.C. Youth League has for the last two

years been mainly confined to the Transvaal. The time has now come for the League to expand throughout and encompass the whole of South Africa including the Protectorates.

All enterprising, progressive and militant youths in all the Provinces of the Union and Protectorates are being asked to commence organising the Youth League in their respective areas or localities.

A NEW FILLIP

We are gratefully indebted to the Transvaal African Students' Association (T.A.S.A.) who, in their recent annual conference at Orlando, Johannesburg, openly declared by a resolution that they are nationalistically oriented and that they therefore whole-heartedly support the A.N.C. Youth League.[22] This gives the Youth League new fillip and new strength. We earnestly hope that the other Provinces will follow suit without delay. Under the banner of Congress African youth will triumphantly march to Freedom   Freedom within our lifetime.

It is depressing, however, to observe that the dragon of hostility against the Youth League is rearing its ugly head. Political careerists and reactionary diehards within and outside Congress, view the Youth League with suspicion. The League is unjustifiably accused of being a parallel organisation to Congress, of planning a coup d'etat, or to seize power in Congress, or to usurp the position of high Congress officials. That is not correct.

It is nothing but a figment of the brain of those pseudo-leaders who are only solicitous about their personal positions, pride and interest and not about the national struggle of the masses. The Youth League is not interested in personalities or positions but in the national struggle.

The League is the product and child of Congress and has no alternative but to carry out the policy and programme of the Mother Body. This cowardly fear of the Youth League is therefore totally unfounded. According to the Youth League's Manifesto, a true leader must be the embodiment or incarnation of the wishes and aspirations of the masses. It is such a leader of the League who pledges its unconditional support and loyalty.

AFRICAN
NATIONAL
CONGRESS
ACTIVITIES

11. A. M. LEMBEDE, "Congress on the March," *Bantu World,* 9 September 1944.

THE AFRICAN National Congress is a fundamental feature of a stage in the evolutionary process of the African people — a stage when the Africans have become conscious of their glorious past, of their fierce present-day struggle for survival and of the great role they can play in, and the substantial contribution they can make to the progress of mankind in the future. This is the African Spirit — the spirit which is being interpreted and applied by the A.N.C.

It can be stated emphatically that the movement is all-inclusive and all-embracing in its organisation. No question of national importance falls outside its precincts. Hence, the problems of African churches, trade unions, teachers, traders, industrialists, farmers and peasants represent merely certain aspects of our colonial national struggle which is one, single and indivisible. It is the great pride of the A.N.C. that it is purely African, and is self-reliant, and self-propelling. To borrow a phrase, "We are paddling our own canoe."

In the past all those forces which endeavoured to demolish the movement dismally failed. But to-day the A.N.C. is facing a formidable alliance or combination of hostile African organisations which are supported or run by Europeans and which aim at destroying the A.N.C. and thus crush and shatter the very soul of the African people. The vain and furious attempt of these organisations is, however, foredoomed to failure. No realistic observer can, however, connive at or conceal some painful facts in the history of the A.N.C. There have been blunders both in policy and execution, there has been now and then a deplorable display of lack of energy and of systematic organisation, but the spirit which is to be interpreted by the A.N.C. is eternal and unchanged.

The progressive policy of the organisation is, to-day, patent to every one; the advancement of the anti-pass campaign;[23] the great financial response given by the Africans to the national sports day organised by Mr. R. G. Baloyi[24] on the 6th August; the considerable rally of Africans of the Northern Transvaal to support the A.N.C. at a huge meeting addressed by Mr. C. S. Ramohanoe (President A.N.C. Transvaal) at Pietersburg a few weeks ago; the progress of Congress organisational

work in the O.F.S. [Orange Free State] and the Cape; the seriousness
with which the Natal Africans view and regard the state of Congress
in that Province; the A.N.C. Youth League which is sounding a trumpet call to mobilise all the national youth forces are examples of the
results achieved.

12. A.M. LEMBEDE, "African National Congress Steady and Satisfactory Progress," *Um-Afrika*, 16 December 1944.

UNDER THE LEADERSHIP of Mr. C. S. Ramohanoe the Transvaal
Congress is energetically pursuing its expansion policy. It is not only
gaining new ground but it is also winning the confidence of the
masses; and strictly speaking, that is the acid test for any great movement.

Congress displayed some initiative in convening a special conference to protest against the banning of open-air meetings. This was on
the 29th October 1944, in Johannesburg. The characteristic feature of
this conference was its representative nature. New branches have
been established at Nigel, Eastern Native Township and other places.
The Congress is just now engaged in a grim battle against the increase of train fares and bus fares.

Recently the President Mr. Ramohanoe addressed a big meeting at
"Tickey Line" Kempton Park Location, and in this meeting the grievances of the people were brought forward, discussed, formulated in
writing and later submitted to the local Town Clerk; these included
insufficience of water supply, lack of grave yard, the threatening
danger of removal of the location; the existence or non existence of
an advisory board. At present the Secretary Mr. D. W. Bopape is offi-
cially touring the Northern Districts of the Transvaal and preaching
the Congress gospel.[25]

One cannot, however, end the expression of appreciation without
sounding a note of warning. There is a serious danger looming large
on the horizon. Congress leaders must be cautious and under no circumstances allow the national movement to be committed into a battle ground of European ideologies, nor allow the national movement
to be dragged into the clash or conflict of these foreign ideologies.

In the titanic war between Stalinites and Trotskyites, we Africanists must maintain an attitude of strict neutrality — of course armed
neutrality. If we are overpowered by an insatiable lust or passion to
indulge in "isms" we have our own "ism" — "Africanism."

The Congress Youth League is also making steady though unobtru-
sive progress. "God bless Africa and her sons and daughters."

13. A. M. LEMBEDE, "Boycott Defended," *Bantu World*, 28 June
1947.

IN THE LAST issue of the "Bantu World," Rev. H. G. Mpitso deprecated the Congress resolutions to boycott all elections under the
Native Representation Act of 1936, and he unleashed an attack which
cannot go unchallenged.[26]

He states: "I am a staunch supporter of the African National
Congress."

Yes, but in many national and provincial conferences of the A.N.C.
and even in local branch meetings, the Rev. Gentleman is often con-
spicuous by his absence.

"Congress leaders should frankly admit that a large number of
those who wield African votes are outside their pale and that they
will vote inspite of its resolutions."

This is a prophetic vision. I thought it was only the Jewish race
which excelled in producing prophets as the Bible shows. It appears,
however, that the African race is a strong rival of the Jews in this type
of day-dreaming about what will happen in future.

"The chiefs, the location advisory boards, the urban and rural elec-
toral colleges owe no allegiance to Congress."

Congress wants no allegiance of government-created bodies. It addresses itself to the African people. It aims at the rally of the African
people. If it succeeds in this, these government-created bodies will
either disappear or fail to function. As for the chiefs they have no
alternative but to support Congress as the recent Prime Minister's
proposals will undermine their position, influence and prestige by
granting extensive powers to the N.R.C. to run the reserves.[27]

SLOGANS REJECTED

"Our leaders should benefit by past failure to implement resolutions passed at mass meetings and adopt different tactics other than pious resolutions. What happened to the resolution passed last year for the burning of passes? Another resolution advised Africans to boycott the Royal visit.[28] Were these resolutions carried out?"

In effect the Rev. Gentleman disapproves and rejects the slogans fraught with human wisdom, slogans that have guided and sustained humanity through centuries and through storms and cyclones of life namely: — "If at first you don't succeed try again"[29] and "failures are often stepping stones to greater things."

Again he says we should adopt different tactics. What tactics? His statement is blank and negative.

BURNING OF PASSES

To refresh the Rev. Gentleman's memory, Congress never passed a resolution to burn passes last year. He is grossly confused.

This shows how isolated and aloof he is from National events; and how indifferent to and ill-informed about Congress activities he is inspite of his claim to be "a staunch Congress supporter."

Furthermore, the Rev. Gentleman would have us believe that because Congress failed to implement certain resolutions in the past therefore it cannot implement any in the future. What a sweeping assumption! Congress is not a stone. It is an organic thing. Like plants and animals, it must grow. Perhaps the Rev. Gentleman will follow me better if I refer to the Bible. St. Paul says: "When I was a child I spoke as a child, thought as a child, acted as a child, but now that I am a man I put away childish things."[30] It may be that Congress is now becoming a man, or reaching maturity.

AFRICAN
NATIONALISM

14. "AFRICANISM," *T.A.S.A. [Transvaal African Students' Association] Bulletin,* I, 2 (July 1944).

ON THE 9TH of April the inaugural meeting of the African Youth League working under the auspices of the African National Congress, was held. Among several brilliant and scholarly speeches, there was one by Mr. A. M. Lembede, B.A., LL.B., on "Africanism," which, in erudition, soared to Himalayan heights.

In his attempt to foster the spirit of nationalism and racial pride, the speaker first dealt with Africa as a continent. He mentioned that it was the mother continent from which America and Australia, according to geological and geographical evidence, must have broken away. The coloured races, he went on to say, were able to live in all types of climates in the torrid, temperate and frigid zones, and were therefore physically superior to the other races which could only live in the temperate zones. Africa's geographical position between the West and the East helped to produce men and women of balanced minds. The West emphasized knowledge and had made great strides in science. But this very knowledge had become self destructive because it enabled them to invent deadly weapons. The East emphasized the spiritual side of life. It was the East which had produced a Mohammed, a Buddha, a Christ; but it was that very spiritualism which had helped to keep the Easterners weak. The numerous religious castes were a negative factor in the progress of the Eastern nations. But Africa, lying between these two extremes, was able to imbibe the spiritualism of the East and the knowledge of the West and produce balanced Africans.

The speaker touched on South African history to focus the attention of the audience upon the sterling qualities of our national heroes. He mentioned men like Hintsa and Ntsikana who had tried for years, fighting against superior weapons, to hurl the White man into the sea. Shaka had tried, by means of the sword, in much the same way as Napoleon, to unite the Black races of Southern Africa. Moshesh, the strategist, had tried by means of kindness, to unite the Basuto tribes into one strong nation.[31]

The speaker ended by saying that the Africans should not import from the West foreign ideologies that do not fit into their culture. They should select only those things which would be helpful to Africans and adapt them to suit African conditions. The Youth League, therefore, aimed at evolving an ideology for Africans, and this would be neither Capitalism, nor Nazism, neither Socialism, nor Communism, but Africanism.

15. A. M. LEMBEDE, "Some Basic Principles of African Nationalism," *Ilanga lase Natal,* 24 February 1945.

(a) THE PHILOSOPHICAL Basis: This can be stated by quoting the words of a famous American writer Thompson: "The materialistic conception of History that conceives of Man as essentially an economic animal — Communism — and the biological interpretation that conceives of him as a beast of Prey — Nazism — are false."[32] Man is body, mind and spirit with needs, desires and aspiration in all three elements of his nature. History is a record of humanity's striving for complete self-realisation.

(b) The Scientific Basis: Charles Darwin the eminent and famous scientist pointed out the profound significance of the law of variation in Nature. One can never find two leaves of plants that are exactly and in all respects the same, nor two stems nor two flowers, nor two animals, nor two human beings nor two nations. Each nation has thus its own peculiar contribution to make towards the general progress and welfare of Mankind. In other words each nation has its own divine mission. Think for instance of the contribution made by the Greeks (Science and philosophy) Romans (law and politics) Jews (Christian religion and technology) French (modern democracy) English (spread of Western civilisation among Non-Europeans throughout the world) Germans (modern science) Russians (modern economic theories) etc. etc. and Africans. "Ex Africa semper quid novi." From Africa always comes something new, said an ancient Latin writer.

(c) Historical basis: It was Paul Kruger who in the gloomy days of the Transvaal Republic said "Wie zich een toekomst scheppen wil, mag het verleden niet uit het oog verliezen." ["Whoever wishes to shape the future should not forget the past."][33]

"One who wants to create the future must not forget the past." These are words of deep human wisdom. We, Africans, have still to erect monuments to commemorate the glorious achievements of our great heroes of the past e.g. Shaka, Moshoeshoe, Hintsa, Sikhukhuni, Khama, Sobhuza, Mozilikazi etc. In their times of environment and under the circumstances in which they lived, these men served their people and did their duty nobly and well. "Lives of great [men] all remind us."[34]

(d) Economic Basis: the fundamental structure of Bantu society is socialistic. There was, for instance, no individual ownership of land in ancient Bantu society. There were no landlords or the so called "absentee" land-lords. Land belonged virtually to the whole tribe and nominally to the King or Chief. Socialism is then our valuable legacy from our ancestors. Our task is to develop this socialism by the infusion of new and modern socialistic ideas.

(e) Democratic Basis: In ancient Bantu society the worth of a man was not assessed by wealth. Any man could rise to any position e.g. of Induna or Captain or general by the virtue of the qualities of courage and ability which were possessed by such man. In our councils or khotlas any citizen could take part in discussions and if a case was being tried anyone could ask questions and cross-examine the accused.[35] The main point is the assessment of human value by moral and spiritual qualities. This is a legacy to be preserved, developed and highly treasured in our hearts.

(f) Ethical Basis: The ethical system of our forefathers was based on ancestor worship. People did certain things or refrained from doing certain things for fear of punishments by the spirits of dead ancestors. We must retain and preserve the belief in the immortality of the spirits of our ancestors but our ethical system today has to be based on Christian morals since there is nothing better anywhere in the world. Morality is the soul of society. Decay and decline of morals brings about the decay and decline of society — so History teaches.

It is only African Nationalism or Africanism that can save the African people. Long live African Nationalism.

16. A. M. LEMBEDE, "Know Thyself," *Bantu World,* 30 June 1945

KNOW THYSELF: These few words pithily synthesise or epitomise the teaching of the ancient Greek philosopher — Socrates — who lived about 400 B.C.

A puzzled, bewildered person may ask: "But why should I know myself? Can't I infer knowledge about myself from the knowledge I have of humanity in general? or from the knowledge of my friends — John, Dick, Lucy and Kate?" The answer is crisply immediate and dogmatic: "No you can't." Although you have much in common with your friends John, Dick, Lucy and Kate — yet you have in your own make-up or inner character something peculiar to yourself which no other human being possesses in the whole cosmos. "Know Thyself."

As it is with individuals, so it is with nations. Each nation has its own peculiar unique character which no other nation in the world possesses or can possess. Each nation has thus its own peculiar talents and potentialities to develop and to realise. Each nation has its own peculiar contribution to make towards the general progress, welfare and happiness of mankind. This eternal law of variations and individual differences among organisms and species was re-discovered and re-emphasized by Charles Darwin about 2,000 years after Socrates.

It is therefore crystal clear that the inevitable conclusion from the above stated propositions is that: it is beyond all limits of possibility that all nations of the world can welcome, accept or adopt one ideology, set of philosophic ideas, or outlook on life. Let us illustrate and support our assertion by a few examples.

RELIGION

The christian [sic] church has vigorously endeavoured to spread and disseminate its doctrines throughout the world. Has it succeeded? No. In Russia, Christian teaching has been practically done away with, and the door has been shut to the church. In India, China, Japan the Christian church has made very little impression. The same may, of course be said of other religions such as Mohamedanism, Hinduism, and Buddhism. Some individuals and nations seem to be impervious to certain religious teachings.

DEMOCRACY

For the last century England and France have been labouring energetically in an attempt to extend, spread and popularise democracy all over the world; sometimes they even went to the extent of forcing it upon other nations. It does not need scholastic learning of History to know that their attempt has not been successful. Fancy what a mockery democracy is in South Africa.

FASCISM

Any comment here is superfluous as the disaster suffered by those who tried to force fascism on the world, is still fresh in our memories.

COMMUNISM

It stands to reason, that any attempt to force or spread communism among all nations of the world will unavoidably meet a similar fate and doom. It will undoubtedly prove fruitless and abortive. What then is the solution to this baffling problem?

Common sense suggests a simple solution — namely that each nation must realise its own potentialities, develop its own talents and retain its own peculiar character, for the benefit of the whole Human Race.

"But" one may retort. "Civilisations grow by borrowing and assimilating some useful material from other civilisations and nations." Quite so. But there is a difference between "borrowing and assimilating" and "being borrowed and assimilated." Yes, the difference may be subtle but it is vast and fundamental.

Africans too, cannot be mere doers and imitators of other nations and their ideologies. Africans can borrow and assimilate what is good from elsewhere but they must at all costs retain and determinedly preserve their own essential character and identity. This is the basic teaching of Africanism and is in line with the ideas of great thinkers, for, with a few exceptions, Socrates and Darwin are the highest peaks of human intelligence. KNOW THYSELF.

17. A. M. LEMBEDE, "National Unity Among Africans," *Ilanga lase Natal,* 6 October 1945

THE FACT that Unity among African tribes is a sine qua non and a prerequisite condition to National Liberation and progress cannot be gainsaid.

This fact becomes plain and indubitable when we consider the approximate populations of various countries of the world as follows: — U.S.A. (130,000,000), Japan (80,000,000), Russia (93,000,000), Germany (80,000,000), England (41,000,000), France (40,000,000), India (350,000,000), China (550,000,000). What is the Union of South Africa with her 10,000,000 inhabitants compared to the above countries?

The necessity for National unity becomes patent and self-evident when one ponders over the approximate populations of some African tribes in South Africa as follows: Xosas [sic] (2,000,000), Zulus (1,500,000), Basuthos [sic] (3,000,000), Swazis (25,000). What can the Xosas alone or Zulus alone or Basuthos alone achieve in comparison with the above-mentioned nations of the world? But in Africa as a whole there are over 150,000,000 Africans, and this compares favourably with other large countries of the world e.g. U.S.A. and Russia.

What is then the right way to Unity and Solidarity among African tribes?

(a) ONE LANGUAGE: Some people imagine that if all African Tribes could speak one language then Unity would be a *fait accompli*. Yes, it is quite true that a single language exercises a unifying influence on a people. But it is not decisive and fundamental. The Swiss Nation speak three languages — German, French, Italian. The Danes and Norwegians speak the same language but they are two different nations; as well as England and U.S.A. If this fact of the power of language were true, then those nations who speak closely related languages would be friendly to one another but it is not necessarily so. Take for instance the Italians, French, and Spaniards; the Chinese and Japanese; the Germans and the Dutch; English itself is a Germanic language.

(b) COLOUR: People of the same colour do sometimes regard themselves as members of the same herd. But this feeling of relatedness is only skin-deep. Otherwise how can we explain the spirit of animosity and national apartness between e.g. the French and the Germans; the Chinese and Japanese? No, the skin is not a decisive factor in nationhood.

(c) INHABITING ONE AND THE SAME COUNTRY: People who live in one and the same Geographical Region tend to be one and homogeneous. But this does not always succeed in creating a nation, as witness, the Dutch and English in South Africa.

(d) COMMON ORIGIN: This does bind and cement peoples but the bond of the cement becomes weaker and weaker with the roll of centuries. We see this illustrated all over the world. What should then be the basis of National Unity?

(e) DOMINATION BY THE SAME SPIRIT: Every Geographical Region is different from other regions climatically, topographically etc. Each region is geographically peculiar and unique. All plants and animals must adapt themselves to a particular region in order to survive. This includes man. In other words plants, animals and man must breathe the spirit of their environment in order to continue living. A region may be a continent. Africa is a region. Now from time immemorial Africa has developed her own peculiar plants, animals and man — the African Native or Aborigine.

The African Natives then live and move and have their being in the spirit of Africa, in short, they are one with Africa. It is then this spirit of Africa which is the common factor of co-operation and the basis of unity among African tribes. It is African Nationalism or Africanism. So that all Africans must be converted from tribalism into African Nationalism which is a higher step or degree of the self-expression and self-realisation of the African spirit. Africa through her spirit is using us to develop that higher quality of Africanism.

We have to go out as apostles to preach the New Gospel of Africanism and to hasten and bring about the birth of a new nation. Such minor insignificant differences of languages, customs etc. will not hinder or stop the irresistible onward surge of the African spirit. This African spirit can realise itself through, and be interpreted by, Africans only. Foreigners of whatever brand and hue can never properly and correctly interpret this spirit owing to its uniqueness, peculiarity and particularity.

18. A. M. LEMBEDE, "Policy of the Congress Youth League," *Inkundla ya Bantu,* May 1946.

THE HISTORY of modern times is the history of nationalism. Nationalism has been tested in the people's struggles and the fires of battle and found to be the only effective weapon the only antidote against foreign rule and modern imperialism. It is for that reason that the great imperialistic powers feverishly endeavour with all their might to discourage and eradicate all nationalistic tendencies among their alien subjects; for that purpose huge and enormous sums of money are lavishly expended on propaganda against nationalism which is dubbed, designated or dismissed as "narrow," "barbarous," "uncultured," "devilish," etc. Some alien subjects become dupes of this sinister propaganda and consequently become tools or instruments of imperialism for which great service they are highly praised, extolled and eulogized by the imperialistic power and showered with such epithets as "cultured," "liberal," "progressive," "Broadminded," etc.

All over the world nationalism is rising in revolt against foreign domination, conquest and oppression in India, in Indonesia, in Egypt, in Persia and several other countries.

Among Africans also clear signs of national awakening, national renaissance or rebirth are noticeable on the far-off horizon.

A new spirit of African nationalism or Africanism, is pervading through and stirring the African society. A young virile nation is in the process of birth and emergence. The national movement imbued with and animated by the national spirit is gaining strength and momentum. The African National Congress Youth League is called upon to aid and participate in this historical process. African nationalism is based on the following cardinal principles.

1. Africa is a blackman's country. Africans are the natives of Africa and they have inhabited Africa, their Motherland, from times immemorial; Africa belongs to them.

2. Africans are one. Out of the heterogeneous tribes, there must emerge a homogeneous nation. The basis of national unity is the nationalistic feeling of the Africans, the feeling of being Africans irrespective of tribal connection, social status, educational attainment or economic class. This nationalistic feeling can only be realised in and interpreted by [a] national movement of which all Africans must be members.

3. The Leader of the Africans will come out of their own loins. No foreigner can ever be a true and genuine leader of the African people because no foreigner can ever truly and genuinely interpret the Afri-

can spirit which is unique and peculiar to Africans only. Some foreigners Asiatic or European who pose as African leaders must be categorically denounced and rejected. An African must lead Africans. Africans must honour, venerate and find inspiration from African heroes of the past, Shaka, Moshoeshoe, Makana, Hintsa, Khama, Mzilikazi, Sekhukhuni, Sobhuza and many others.

4. Co-operation between Africans and other Non-Europeans on common problems and issues may be highly desirable. But this occasional co-operation can only take place between Africans as a single unit and other non-European groups as separate units. Non-European unity is a fantastic dream which has no foundation in reality.

5. The divine destiny of the African people is National Freedom. Unless Africans achieve national freedom as early as possible they will be confronted with the impending doom and imminent catastrophe of extermination; they will not be able to survive the satanic forces economic, social and political, unleashed against them. Africans are being mowed down by such diseases as tuberculosis, typhus, venereal diseases etc. Infantile mortality is tremendously high. Moral and physical degeneration is assuming alarming dimensions. Moral and spiritual degeneration manifests itself in such abnormal and pathological phenomena as loss of self-confidence, inferiority complex, a feeling of frustration, the worship and idolisation of whitemen, foreign leaders and ideologies. All these are symptoms of a pathological state of mind.

As a result of the educational and industrial colour bar, young African men and women are converted into juvenile delinquents.

Now the panacea of all these ills is National Freedom. In as much as, when Africans are free, they will be in a position to pilot their own ship and, unhampered, work toward their own destiny and, without external hindrance or restriction devise ways and means of saving or rescuing their perishing race.

Freedom is an indispensable condition for all progress and development. It will only be when Africans are free that they will be able to exploit fully and bring to fruition their divine talent and contribute something new towards the general welfare and prosperity of Mankind; and it will only be then that Africans will enter on a footing of equality with other nations of the world into the commonwealth of nations; and only then will Africans occupy their rightful and honourable place among the nations of the world.

6. Africans must aim at national progress or advancement. We must guard against the temptation of lop-sided or one-sided progress. Our forces as it were, must march forward in a co-ordinated manner and in all theatres of the war socially, educationally, culturally, morally, economically, and politically. Hence the Youth League must be all-inclusive.

7. After national freedom, then, socialism. Africans are naturally socialistic as illustrated in their social practices and customs. The achievement of national liberation will therefore herald or usher in a new era of African socialism. Our immediate task however is not socialism but national liberation.

Our Motto: Freedom In Our Lifetime.

19. A. M. LEMBEDE, "National Units," *Ilanga lase Natal,* 18 May 1946.

THERE IS practically some unanimity and consensus of opinion amongst African leaders concerning the necessity of National Unity among Africans. The realisation that National Unity is a prerequisite condition, a sine qua non of National Freedom has gained ground considerably. But there still prevails immense confusion as to the mode or method of achieving it. After reading this article I hope this confusion will evaporate and disappear like the morning mist.

Our National Unity then consists of two essential elements namely Tribal synthesis and organisational or ideological solidarity.

(a) Tribal Synthesis — by this we mean the creation of a homogenous nation out of heterogeneous tribes. History is a process — ever moving, ever changing, ever developing. Even before the advent of Europeans into this country, tribal synthesis was in the process of developing. It would be achieved by force of arms, by the spear. Shaka is a good example of an African who was inspired by the flaming passion to unify the whole of black Africa, through the instrumentality of the spear. He succeeded excellently in Natal. This process of growth and development was interrupted or rather diverted by the arrival of Europeans. It was not stopped however because Europeans brought with them a new driving force, a new mainspring of tribal synthesis namely oppression. This force is now carrying on where Shaka left off. Africans today, owing to common suffering, are outgrowing and transcending the primitive, narrow, petty tribal limits and differences and are recognising themselves and one another as Africans, first and foremost. In other words Africanism is striking root and the feeling of consanguinity and fraternity is growing apace. Only a few dwarfish stunted and antiquated individuals still cling tenaciously to tribalism, but they are far behind times and their influence will gradually wane and vanish as the great march of the African people moves forward by leaps and bounds.

(b) Organisational Solidarity

We may achieve tribal synthesis and yet still lack national unity. This phenomenon occurs when a nation is divided or split organisationally or ideologically. This deplorable state of affairs naturally leads to internecine strifes and civil wars, as witness, the recent civil wars in Spain and China.

Some African Leaders whose beclouded minds are specially framed for the perversion of truth and misinterpretation of reality believe, for instance that African National Unity can be achieved by conglomerating, building or crowding together such organisations as the African National Congress, African Democratic Party,[36] Fourth International,[37] Communist Party etc. They naively believe and frivolously maintain that these organisations can work harmoniously together. That is nothing other than childish simplicity. That harmonious co-operation cannot be achieved among and between these warring organisations has been manifestly demonstrated by the failure and fiasco of the recent Anti-Pass Campaign.

How then can Unity be achieved in this case? In this case Unity can be achieved only through one of the organisations gaining power and ascendancy over others and finally destroying and annihilating all the others. This is the only way which has been well proved in practice and extensively utilised by Nature herself. Organisational and ideological Unity for us can only be found in one single movement — the National Movement.

In conclusion we must re-emphasise that tribal synthesis and organisational and ideological solidarity are essential and indispensable
for national unity.

It will only be after we have achieved our national unity and gained
our freedom that we shall be able to enter on a footing of equality
with other nations of the world into the International society or
commonwealth of nations.

20. A. M. LEMBEDE, "In Defence of Nationalism," *Inkundla ya
Bantu,* 27 February 1947.

"MY REACTION to India was often an emotional one . . . It
took the form of nationalism. . . . nationalism was and is inevitable
in the India of my day; it is a natural and healthy growth. For any
subject country national freedom must be the first and dominant
urge. Recent events all over the world have demonstrated that the
notion that nationalism is fading away before the impact of internationalism and proletarian movement has little truth," (Jawaharlal
Nehru: *The Discovery of India,* 1945, page 32).[38] This unique statement made by one of the greatest men of modern times, is pregnant
with profound significance for all Africans for, by substituting "Africa"
for "India" this statement would apply aptly and crisply to African
Nationalism or Africanism.

African Nationalism (which by the way has become a nightmare to
some prominent liberal European and African politicians in this country) will sweep away all vestiges of tribalism and unify all Africans.
The tie that will bind all Africans together under the banner of Africanism will be the passionate and glowing love for Africa — our
motherland — and her Freedom. Mazzini,[39] appealing to his countrymen in 1848 said: "Love your country. Your country is the land
where your parents sleep, where is spoken that language in which the
chosen of your heart, blushing, whispered the first word of love; it is
the home which God has given you, that by striving to perfect yourselves therein, you may prepare to ascend to Him. It is your name;
your glory, your sign among the people. Give to it your thoughts, your

counsels, your blood. Raise it up great and beautiful — and see that you leave it uncontaminated by any trace of falsehood or servitude; unprofaned by dismemberment." Oh! if these inspiring words could sink and soak into our minds and hearts!

African Nationalism is to be pursued with the fanaticism and bigotry of religion, for it is the only creed that will dispel and disperse the inferiority complex which blurs our sight and darkens our horizon. The inferiority complex is a psychological malady; the opium that dulls our mental faculties and represses our physical energy. We must therefore verily believe that we are inferior to no other race on earth; that Africa and ourselves are one, that we have a divine mission of unifying and liberating Africa thus enabling her to occupy her rightful and honourable place amongst the nations of the world. We must develop race pride.

The dynamic human energy that will be released by African nationalism will be more powerful and devastating in its effects than the atomic energy.

21. A. M. LEMBEDE, "African Nationalism and the New African Masses," *Ilanga lase Natal,* 21 June 1947.

NATIONALISM IS essentially an ideology of the masses because it stirs the deepest human feelings. The African masses today are becoming imbued with the spirit of nationalism. This can be clearly seen in the new tendencies and orientation of the African National Congress. The African people through African National Congress have fully supported the indefinite adjournment of the Native Representative Council and have categorically rejected the recent Smuts' tentative proposals to the six members of the Native Representative Council at Cape Town and have taken a grave decision to boycott all future elections under the Native Representative Act of 1936. In rural areas Africans demand more land and strongly resist Government plans for the limitation of stock. In urban areas, through the shanty town movements, Africans demand more land on which to build their own houses. At last there is likely to emerge a concerted struggle of the African Urban and Rural populations. The cry of both is "we want land."

This demand for more land forms the basis for the more urgent and pressing demand for national freedom and liberation that is, for full franchise and citizenship in the land of our birth.

Today Africans are threatened or menaced by the hideous spectre of gradual but certain extermination as a race. Ravaging diseases such as T.B. [tuberculosis] claim about 30,000 Africans victims every year.[40] Infantile mortality is so high that about half of all the children born die in infancy. The African Society stands in danger of social and moral disintegration caused by immorality and hooliganism which are assuming disquieting proportions. About one-fourth of the African people constitute the temporary or permanent prison population. All these things are symptoms of social ills or pathological state of the present Bantu Society caused by political oppression and economic exploitation of the Africans, by the so-called "trustees of the African people." There is only one cure for all these ills namely the overthrow of oppression in this country and the free participation of Africans in the government of the land. When Africans achieve their national freedom and are able to legislate and make laws for themselves all these ills and anomalies will vanish into thin air like a morning mist.

Europeans are closing ranks in order to intensify and defend the policy of colour segregation and discrimination in this country, and in order to ward off what they style the African menace to "White Civilisation" e.g. the Malan-Havenga co-operation pact.[41] This is a serious challenge to Africans also to close ranks and stand together. Away with tribalism! Away with the multiplicity of African organisations. The African National Congress must negotiate with the All-African Convention[42] and other purely African Organisations for closer co-operation. All purely African organisations which do not differ in principle ought to march forward together either in unity or partnership.

"White Civilisation" as understood by the Whites in South Africa namely Colour Superiority, discrimination and oppression, has no future in Africa; but Western Culture and civilisation in the form of science, art, philosophy, has a longer future than we can imagine in this continent, for, the latter, although to a great extent developed by Europeans, is yet a legacy, a heritage of the whole human race. It is the common property of humanity as a whole. No section of Mankind has the right selfishly to keep or reserve this to itself.

African Nationalism then aims at a united progressive respectably

African nation. Its forward march is inevitable and irresistible, in the words of Pandit Nehru: "To defend the Status Quo is to surrender." Africans must move forward to freedom.

"Die tyd vir mooipraat is verby,
En mooipraat is nie meer die plan;
'n Plekkie in die son vir my —
Die regte van 'n vrye man!"[43]

22. A. M. LEMBEDE, "Why General Smuts' Proposals Will Be Rejected," *African Advocate,* July 1947.

ARISTOTLE, an ancient Greek philosopher, defined man as a "rational animal." Man is an animal, but only distinguished from other animals by his possession of mind, intellect or reason. The most scientific definition of man still stands unchanged today. It is thus evident that skin pigmentation is not the essence of man. In South Africa, however, more than in any other country in the World, the colour of man's skin is worshipped, idolised and adopted as an essential mark or criterion of human superiority and inferiority. The philosophy of colour-worship has no scientific foundation whatsoever. It is a nefarious, devilish ideology which at present is unfortunately dominating and holding sway over the minds of most Europeans in this country. Africans are, according to this ideology, regarded as inferior creatures, incapable of higher education, of helping themselves, of governing themselves, and even of knowing what is good for themselves. In short, Africans are looked upon as ape-men, imbeciles, infants, [and] barbarians. Hence the colour-bar laws of the Union, aiming at colour discrimination, oppression of and discrimination against Africans. This is euphemistically called Trusteeship. Now this colour ideology is a serious menace to the existence or survival of Africans as a race. According to my conservative estimation, the African population of the Union shall be wiped off or exterminated within 5000 years from today.

Where are the Bushmen? Where are the Hottentots [sic]? There are already visible unmistakable signs and indications that [they] are a dying, a disappearing, a perishing race.

Physical deterioration, high infantile mortality, high general death rate (Tuberculosis and venereal diseases), moral and social decay and disintegration of Bantu society (loose morals, hooliganism, Juvenile delinquency), gross illiteracy, dire poverty — all these phenomena point in one direction: extinction of the Bantu race.

Dr. Gluckman, Minister of Health, recently pointed out that tuberculosis is caused by poor economic and social living conditions, but did not suggest a remedy to ameliorate this heart-rending state of affairs. The remedy is of course obvious. Africans must achieve political freedom and be directly represented in all state organs that make laws so as to make laws to facilitate their own economic advancement and for their own social security. Only by that remedy can the African race be served or reserved.

Such measures as are suggested by the Prime Minister will only accelerate and not even delay our approaching racial disaster and extermination.

In order to secure the continued existence or survival of Africans as a people the colour ideology must be smashed and overthrown.

The grim struggle for the overthrow of this ideology will demand of us an unshakeable will-power and resolute determination with an unwavering [faith] in our divine destiny which is national freedom.

Should we fail or falter in this gigantic struggle, then our future generation[s] will pass a verdict of guilt on us. We shall be cursed by our children.

Non-European races all over the world are clamoring for freedom — India, Indonesia, Egypt, Madagascar. Gandhi has already cautioned Europe that the future of mankind does not lie with the white races. If Africans strive for national liberation, they are therefore participating in a colossal struggle for human freedom and they are comrades in arms of the majority of the human race.

The last session of the UNO [United Nations] already demonstrated that the era of colour domination and discrimination has passed never to return. White South Africa is disillusioned with and embittered against this new international attitude to the religion of colour-worship.

She is weeping on the ruins of the past. It appears that General Smuts is preparing for the next Uno session next September and he wants to convince the "prejudiced" "ill-informed" outside world as to how much the Union has done for the Natives. We maintain that the world must know the truth. We want no "bone to chew." We want meat. We are not dogs.

General Smuts proposes to give the N.R.C. Executive powers. In other words, we are being asked to commit suicide, to administer our own self-destruction or oppression under the existing colour-bars of the Country.

Furthermore, the Prime Minister intends to invest the Native Representative Council with powers to control and administer the Native reserves. Everyone knows that the Government is rapidly becoming unpopular in the reserves because instead of providing more land, [it] is calling upon the people to limit their stock. Hence, the delegation of this unpleasant task to the Natives themselves.

Again the action of conferring upon the Natives' Representative Council extensive powers to administer or govern reserves will deal a battering blow to the powers and prestige of African Chiefs in the reserves.

Moreover the plea of a Government within a Government or of two parallel Governments within the same state, is a political absurdity.

The shortest line between two points is [a] straight line. Let the Prime Minister amend the South Africa Act so as to include Africans as Council citizens of South Africa with full franchise. That is all.

Oh! Almighty God! how long shall we be humiliated, insulted and sworn at because of our colour which you giver of all gifts — gave to us?

23. "LAST MESSAGE OF LATE MR. A. M. LEMBEDE, MA., LL.B.," *African Advocate,* August/September, 1947.

ADDRESSING A gathering in Leake Hall, Orlando, on Sunday, 27th June, 1947, at a reception organised by the A.N.C.Y.L. in honour of Mr. A. Mda, B.A., lecturer at the Roma University and formerly organising secretary of the Congress Youth League, Mr. A. Lembede,

M.A., LL.B., recalled the stirring words of a great scholar and publicist: "Man is born free," he said, "and everywhere he is in chains."[44]

"The history of Mankind," Mr. Lembede continued, "is the history of the liberation of Mankind."

"Throughout the ages, man has fought and struggled to free himself from one kind of serfdom or another. The history of man to emancipate himself from slavery by man is well known. It is the story of Europe after the French Revolution, of England after 1215, of South Africa after 1833, of Russia after 1917, of India, Egypt and Indonesia to-day."

Mr. Lembede pointed out that man is still in bondage to a colour slavery from which it becomes the duty of man to liberate himself still.

"In Africa this bondage to a colour slavery is attendant with complexes of superiority and inferiority, complexes and contentions that are grave to the African himself.

"Nature has endowed the African with all the elements of power, of creation and of nobility."

"It is the duty of the African, who at one time was judged by those who professed knowledge, to be incapable of attaining to a J.C. [Junior Certificate] academic standard, not to allow himself to be swamped by the tide of doctrines of inferiority.

"The African has passed his J.C., his Matriculation, and, like Mr. Mda to whom we pay tribute to-day, the African has succeeded in his degree examinations, in Arts, in Science, in Law."

"Africa must, after what has been a long lull, surge forward to conquer knowledge and the World."

"The roots of civilisation are deep in the soil of Africa. Egypt is the cradle of civilisation not only in the sciences but even in the matter of shaving. Hannibal, conqueror and polygamist, had three black African wives; Moses married an African; neither Europe nor Asia is devoid of African blood. Christ himself, at a young age, found protection in Africa. On His way to Calvary his support came from Africa.

"Africans have played a role in history, a role that now they cannot deny themselves of or be denied. Here is a vision: "To fight for liberation, to fight in defence of the greatness and nobility of the sons and daughters of Africa."

RELIGION
AND
CHURCHES

24. A. M. LEMBEDE, "African National Congress and Churches,"
Umteteli wa Bantu, 29 July 1944

IN THEIR spiritual make-up, the Africans exhibit indications of striking affinity to the people of the Orient, i.e., Asiatics. Africans are a deeply religious people. To them the doctrines of Christ, Mahomed, Buddha, Confucius, do not sound strange, queer or foreign. This explains our eager and ready acceptance and adoption of Christianity. It is a deplorable distortion of facts to say that Africans did not know God before the advent of the Europeans to this country.

By adopting Christianity we have not suddenly discovered a new God; what has happened is that our old conception of Deity has become clearer and better defined.

Our religious feeling is to be treasured as of supreme value in our national struggle, because, like the Israelites of old, we shall achieve national consolidation and progress only when we become conscious of our divine mission and destiny.

This consciousness has already revealed itself in the African National Congress. Most African churches have given their wholehearted support to the Congress. As a matter of fact many outstanding Congress leaders have been ministers of religion, e.g., Rev. Mr. Dube,[45] Rev. Mr. Mahabane[46] and many others.

Even today, in our Transvaal African National Congress, we have Revs. Mookie[47] [*sic*], Tema,[48] Tantsi[49] and others. The African National Congress and the African Churches are inseparable.

But today there is a great danger looming large on the far-off horizon. A hundred and one political parties are springing up like mushrooms. Some of these parties want to exploit the Africans' religious feeling for party purposes.

The Africans must be on the qui vive; they must watch carefully and resist these tendencies. Our religious feeling is a treasure of our souls; we have received it from our ancestors and we are constrained and in duty bound to pass it on, untarnished, to the coming generations.

25. A. M. LEMBEDE, "The Conception of God as Expounded by or as it Emerges from the Writings of Great Philosophers —

From Descartes to the Present Day," M.A. Thesis, 1945. University of South Africa.

In 1943 Lembede registered for a M.A. thesis in Philosophy at the University of South Africa. His fifty-two page thesis, accepted in 1945, traced the concept of God from the Greek philosophers to modern philosophers such as Descartes, Leibniz, Spinoza, Hume, Kant, Hegel, and William James. We have excerpted portions of his thesis that reflect his personal thinking on religion.

CHAPTER IX
SCIENCE ON THE OFFENSIVE

"We thus arrive at the paradoxical conception
of God as a gaseous vertebrate."
— Haeckel

"Religion is the opium of the people."
— Karl Marx

At this stage it appears proper and fitting that we make a short pause and cast our glance aside and cursorily and briefly examine the influence of Science on the conception of God, especially because scientific ideas and outlooks permeate, to a very great extent, the speculation of modern philosophers.

Science tends to create or encourage a materialistic "weltaanschauung." We observe this phenomenon, for instance, in ancient Greece during the time of Democritus and other Greek scientists. We notice the same also with Hobbes in the 16th century and with the Encyclopedists in the 17th and 18th centuries. It is also the case with modern scientists. Hence science is often interpreted as being anti-religious or atheistic. The devastating attack of science on religion is directed on or aimed at a personal God or anthropomorphic deity. It dismisses religion based on such a god, as a superstition, a myth, a relic or vestige of our primitive and barbaric past. It may be stated also that an attack on the human spirit or soul; or a materialistic interpretation thereof, has far-reaching repercussions in religion and the conception of God. Let us support our proposition by reference to some specific sciences.

(a) *The Influence of Biology.*

Charles Darwin (1817–1882) is generally regarded as the founder of modern evolutionist Biology. In his study of plants and animals, Darwin was struck by the fact that in the whole world not two leaves or plants are the same or perfectly similar in structure, no two flowers, no two animals, no two human beings. Again, in nature, we find several species of plants or animals belonging to the same genus. To the genus man, for instance, belong Chinese, Africans, Europeans, and so on; in the same way, there are several species of maize, wheat, birds, cattle and so forth.

Before the time of Darwin it was generally believed that such species had been separately created by God. Darwin set out to disprove this theory of separate creation of species. He pointed out that every individual or species possesses some variations which distinguish that individual or species from every other individual or species; and that these variations are beneficial to the possessor as they enable it to adapt itself to the environment and thus to survive in the struggle for existence against other individuals which do not possess those particular variations. The latter perish or are exterminated. Now these beneficial variations are, according to the principle of heredity, passed from generation to generation and become more accentuated in each generation. This is the theory of natural selection, by which new individuals and new species are evolved. Man himself has been evolved from lower animals by the same process. It is here where Darwin's theory becomes diametrically opposed to the biblical story of creation as narrated in the Book of Genesis. Darwin's theory dismisses the idea of God who is a direct creator of plants, animals and man.

Haeckel (1899), basing his arguments on the theory of evolution, traces the gradual historical evolution of the human soul from the animal soul. He then goes on to denounce the anthropomorphic conception of God and points out that the personal anthropomorphism of God has become so natural to the majority of believers that they experience no shock when they find God personified in human form, in picture and statue and in the varied images of the poet in which God takes human form — that is, changed into a vertebrate. Although God is conceived as an immaterial spirit, yet He is not conceived to be incorporeal but merely invisible, gaseous.

(b) *The Influence of Chemistry*

Dr. Broad in his book "The Mind and Its Place in Nature" (published 1937) elaborates an interpretation of the human soul in terms or after the analogy of chemical compounds. If, for instance, one mixes hydrogen and oxygen in a certain proportion a chemical compound called water results. By the knowledge of hydrogen alone or oxygen alone no one could predict the fact that if these two elements are mixed in a certain proportion, the compound would be water. This can only be known or learnt after it has taken place.

After water emerges from a certain mixture of hydrogen and oxygen, in a similar manner the human soul emerges from the chemical mixture of elements in the human body and brain. From the observation of the elements alone, no one could know that their mixture or combination in a certain manner would result in the formation or emergence of the human soul. ". . . The characteristic behaviour of the whole could not even in theory be deduced from the most complete knowledge of the behaviour of its components taken separately or in other combinations and of their proportions and arrangements in this whole."*

If the soul of man is an emergent from or a compound of chemical elements, then obviously the idea of a God who created a man and breathed the soul into his nostrils — in other words a personal God and Creator — becomes superfluous. There is no place for such a god.

(c) *Marxism*

Karl Marx (1818-1885) sought to explain the human soul and the economic institutions in materialistic terms. To him, the basic or fundamental reality is matter. Spirit or soul is a product of matter. "The material, sensuously perceptible world to which we belong, is the only reality. Our consciousness and thinking, however, supra sensuous as they may seem, are the product of mind, but mind itself is merely the highest product of matter."** Lenin says, "The world itself is merely the highest product of how matter moves and of how matter thinks."***

---

* Broad: *Mind and Its Place in Nature*, p. 59.
** Karl Marx: in Stalin's "Dialectical and Historical Materialism."
*** Lenin: Ibid.

The origins of religion and the belief in the gods is ascribable to two sources. Firstly, "fear created the gods." — the fear of the mysterious and apparently inscrutable and awe-inspiring forces and phenomena of Nature around us and the fear of death.

Secondly, religion is the instrument by which the well-to-do, privileged class (capitalists) lull to sleep and keep in subjection the lower exploited class (proletariat) in that religion teaches the proletariat to acquiesce in and be satisfied with its lot of toiling, misery, and dire poverty, with the hope of finding happiness and inheriting life everlasting in a legendary or mythical heaven. Religion is thus applied on the oppressed masses as a drug, an intoxicant, an opium. Marx exclaims: "Religion is the opium of the people" and Lenin adds: "This postulate is the cornerstone of the whole philosophy of marxism with regard to religion."* "No amount of reading matter, however enlightened, will eradicate religion from those masses who are crushed by the grinding toil of capitalism and subjected to the blind, destructive forces of capitalism until the masses themselves learn to fight against the social facts from which religion arises in a united disciplined, planned and conscious manner — until they learn to fight against the rule of capitalists in all its forms."** According to this theory, God is merely a complex of ideas engendered by the ignorance of mankind and by its subjection firstly beneath the forces of nature, and secondly, by class oppression. By spreading and disseminating scientific knowledge among the masses and by abolishing social classes, religion and belief in the gods will automatically disappear.

Dr. Diederichs criticises this conception of God and religion and points out that it deplorably overlooks another source of religion or belief, namely, the problem of human suffering which cannot be removed, abolished, or done away with, even in an ideal classless society. "Wat die Kommunis oor die hoof sien is die bronne van lyding wat in die individu alleen gelee is asook sulkes wat tot die wese van alle eindigheid behoort. Sal in die kommunistiese samelewing nie meer so iets bestaan as siekte en dood nie, sal daar meer so iets wees as sielesmart, gewetenswroeging nie?"***

Even when we are happy, we need somebody superhuman to whom

* Lenin: *On Religion,* p. 16 (Little Lenin Library, Vol. VII)
** Lenin: Ibid, p. 20.
*** Diederichs: *Die Kommunism,* pp. 115-116.

we can express our gratitude for our joy, hilarity, and mirth. "Behalwe die weg van lyding, is daar nog n' ander weg wat tot God voer nl. die weg van ons vreugde en van ons dankbaarheid."*

We may also add, and draw attention to, the words of the poet Guido Geselle:[50]

"Daar huivert on —
Weerstaanbaar iets
In 's menschen merg en midden, —
Dat hemelwaards
De ziele haalt,
Dat knielen doet en bidden."

CHAPTER XII
CONCLUSION

"Rock of ages cleft for me."
    — Hymn

"Per omnia saecula saeculorum."
    — Latin Prayer

I have now come to the end of my cursory survey of the ideas of great philosophers, from Descartes to the present day. Of course, I have selected only those ideas which to my mind illustrate or elucidate the conception of God according to the philosophical systems of different philosophers.

It should be mentioned, that several philosophers are omitted — not because they are unimportant or because there is nothing about God expressly stated or implied in their writings — but because there are so many philosophers that, to include them all, would perhaps make this dissertation undesirably long. I have, for instance, omitted Bertrand Russell who seems to find ultimate reality in the laws of pure logic and mathematics — laws which are valid and operate throughout the universe.

No mention also has been made about the philosopher Nietzsche who dismisses Christianity as slave-morality and holds that Power or the will to power is the ultimate reality or God.

Two propositions have been established. Firstly, that the growth

---

* Diederichs: Ibid. p. 116.

and spread of knowledge and science is incompatible with or subversive of the personal or anthropomorphic conception of god. History repeats itself. What happened in ancient Greece is again taking place in the modern world. It is not necessary to elaborate this point any further as the preceding Chapters have made it clear and plain.

The second proposition is this, that practically all philosophers we have studied do not, in reality and in fact, deny the existence of God. They only differ as to the conception of God. The fierce strife among them is not raging on the existence of God, but on His essence. His qualities and attributes — on who He is; on the "What" of God and not on His "that," to borrow two words from Bradley. To Descartes God is a perfect spiritual being; to Spinoza, an all-inclusive universal substance; to Leibniz, a supreme spiritual monad; to Berkeley, an active creative spirit; to Kant, a guarantee of our happiness, freedom, and immortality; to Hegel, an all-inclusive Absolute; to Karl Marx, material economic progress; to Alexander, the whole universe in the process of creating deity, and so on.

The conflict between Religion and Science can be resolved. Religion and Science are not irreconcilably opposed to each other. Religion should remember that as the human mind progresses and explores uncharted regions of knowledge, human ideas are born, mature and "senesce." So that to keep up with the times, religion must be constantly brushing aside or discarding its old antiquated ideas, practices and crudities which belonged to the infant stage of the human race. Science, on the other hand, must refrain from its usual wild, dogmatic assertions about those things which we do not as yet clearly and distinctly perceive and conceive.

EPILOGUE
GOD AS THE SELF-REALISATION
OF THE EVOLVING UNIVERSE

"The consciousness of the divine may
come to us as the law or direction of
our life — the nisus of our historic and
individual striving; the nisus . . . towards
the highest level which we call God."
— Boodin

"The more deeply harmonised are a man's faculties
of feeling and thought, the finer and more
fundamental are his powers of achieving contact
with reality."
                              — Fausset

"Reality then . . . is truly known to be a
connected and self-consistent, or internally
coherent system."
                              — Taylor

After studying the God-idea as expounded by several great philosophers, I think I should, with modesty, state my own view — with
modesty because "fools rush in where angels fear to tread."

God may be conceived, not as a person or thing; or as a perfect and
already existing being, but as a state towards which the whole universe is gradually moving. This state is an absolute harmony of all the
elements of the universe. The progressive movement is a gradual
achievement of greater and greater harmony.

We know from our own human nature that things which give us
the true and enduring pleasure or happiness are those which display
or manifest the characteristic of being harmonious constituted, as
witness the objects of art — a statue, a song, a poem.

The value of a great scientific idea or invention lies in this, that it
brings about harmony in things or between things and ourselves, in
the place of previously existing discord, disharmony and confusion.

I deeply admire the Christian "hypothesis" which has, for about
two thousand years, helped to create harmony between man and his
environment — material and human, for, it tells us that there is God
who created heaven and earth and all that is therein — the ant, the
lion, tree, sun, man, and all other existents. It teaches that God loves
us, He forgives us our trespasses; that our souls emanated from Him
and are immortal; that after death we shall live in eternal happiness
with God in heaven if we have been good here on earth. These ideas
give to ordinary men and women rest and satisfaction; they enable us
to go on with our daily work and routine without worrying as to what
all these things around us mean. I think all religions — primitive and
modern — are an attempt to create harmony between man and the

world, for in the long run we can only rest and experience satisfaction in harmony.

God is a state of harmony which the world is in process of realising. The highest achievement of this cosmic process is, so far, the evolution of man who is the best specimen we have, of the universal or absolute harmony, still to be achieved. There is harmony between human mind and body. Man's great task is to shape, mould, and render harmonious the elements or parts of the universe.

Science is concerned mainly with knowledge: religion, with feeling. Science and religion can be harmonised by right action. Now the perfect harmony of religion, science, and right action, can only be realised in the Absolute Harmony — God. Today these three entities are still far from being harmonised. We have knowledge, but we misapply it because we do not possess the right feeling. Sometimes we have the right feeling and true knowledge, but we lack power to act rightly, we lack will power.

The existence of matter or material objects as opposed to, or apart and separate from, mind, is due to our failure, so far, to create harmony in the world. Hence there arises the discord between mind and matter — the latter being the not yet assimilated part of the universe. The discord also between knowledge, feeling, and willing, or between science and religion, is traceable to the same cause, so that the conquest of matter by mind, as, for instance, in the annihilation of distance by trains, aeroplanes, radio, television; and the development and refinement of human feeling by higher and more sublime forms of religion and ethics and the right powerful action to create harmony — this is our highest calling.

A true system of philosophy, to my mind, must account for and explain all aspects of human nature. A philosophy which lays stress on either the cognitive or sentimental or volitional aspect to the neglect or exclusion of other aspects; or a philosophy which regards man as merely and purely cognitive and ignores or overlooks the volitional and affective aspects of human nature or pretends that these aspects are non-existent — such a philosophy, in my opinion, is deficient and inadequate. In man there is something of a blind force and the feeling of longing and yearning for something higher and better than ourselves.

Our great values, namely, truth, goodness, and beauty — themselves forms of harmony and ultimately one and single harmony — are, as it were, beacons pointing for us the way to Absolute Harmony — God.

26. A. M. LEMBEDE, "African Nationalism and the Christian Church," *Ilanga lase Natal,"* 22 September 1945.

AFRICANS ARE essentially a spiritual and religious people. They believe in the spiritual reality which is the foundation beneath the material phenomena of the visible world. Even in their old ancestor-worship, Africans fanatically believed in the community and communion of the living and the dead. In other words they believed in the immortality of the human soul.

In their spiritualism, Africans exhibit striking affinity to the people of the East. The ascetic and mystical religious life of a Christ, a Buddha, a Confucius, a Hindu saint, a Japanese saint do not sound strange to the African.

Obviously, the materialism — the doctrine that matter is the fundamental essence the fons et origo, of the Cosmos and that spirit is merely a superfluous by-product of matter — will never be accepted or adopted by the majority of the African people.

We need Christianity for its sublime and lofty ethical values. Morality is the soul of society. Without sound morals a society must inevitably gravitate to low levels of beastly existence — so History teaches.

Some eminent thinkers have one-sidedly given prominence to or laid emphasis on the weaknesses, errors and imperfections of Christianity and designated it as Slave-morality "Opium of the people" etc. But to my mind, the essence of Christianity is not submissiveness, meekness, resignation to the sinister and base order of society characterised by exploitation and oppression of the underdog. No the essence of Christianity is Calvary, or the Cross — the ready willingness to offer and sacrifice one's life at the altar of one's own convictions, for the benefit of one's fellowmen. This is revolutionary doctrine. We should accordingly understand that the path of the Africans to their

National emancipation and progress is the path of the cross and this is in many respects analogous to the path of Christ carrying the heavy cross from Pilate's Palace to Mount Calvary.

Africanism or African nationalism fully realises the importance of Christianity in our national struggle; hence African nationalism will protect defend and espouse the cause of Christianity. Correspondingly, it is the bounden duty of all African Churches to rally round the banner of African Nationalism. The church should do this for the sake of its own preservation; for there are satanic forces that have been unleashed in the world today with the malicious and malignant purpose of undermining destroying or demolishing the Christian faith and doctrine.

DEBATES AND RELATIONS WITH OTHER ORGANIZATIONS

27. "HITLER'S NEW CONVERT," *Inkululeko,* 9 September 1944.

HITLER IS rapidly losing all his supporters in Europe. The rats
are leaving the sinking ship. But he appears to have found a new recruit in the ranks of the African National Congress.

A correspondent who was present at the recent Congress meeting
in Orlando writes criticising the speech made there by Mr. Lembede.

"He spoke firmly but like a qualified Nazi. He condemned every
organisation which had Europeans in its ranks and lashed the Jews in
the most vicious terms. In fact if one were to close one's eyes when he
was speaking, one would certainly think one was listening to Hitler
broadcasting from Berlin." My correspondent, himself a leading and
distinguished Congressman comments: "Only a poor politician or an
inexperienced nationalist would make such an attack on other organisations. Perhaps our 'intelligent' friend will yet learn by bitter experience if not by the experience of others, that to attack enemies and
friends alike is national suicide."

28. "MR. LEMBEDE REPLIES," *Inkululeko,* 23 September 1944.

I HAVE noted with great surprise and disappointment the unprovoked vitriolic and virulent attack on me by the "Inkululeko" in its
issue of 9th September 1944, under the heading, "Hitler's New Convert."[51]

The said article refers to a Congress meeting held at Orlando on
the 13th August, 1944. It says that in that meeting I spoke "like a qualified Nazi" and goes further "if one were to close one's eyes when he
was speaking one would certainly think one was listening to Hitler's
broadcasting from Berlin."

The said article identifies or associates me with the arch enemies
of this country, and the probable result of that may be that I shall be
exposed to the peril of internment or deportation. Were you aware of
that, Mr. Editor? I do not think it was your intention at all.

Again the said article states that "I lashed the Jews in the most
vicious terms." This statement can be dismissed as a laughable and
distorted exaggeration. What is meant by vicious?

What I did, Sir, was to denounce all white people who pretend to be or pose as the leaders of the African people. "The leaders of a nation come out of its loins," so history teaches.

We cannot acquiesce in the political confusion occasioned by some white men who start or run some African political organisations which divide the Africans and render them helpless and impotent. It is immaterial whether such white men are English, Dutch, German or Jew. In the Orlando meeting I made mention of [. . .] Englishmen and Dutchmen and Jews. I was not conscious of the fact that the mention of the Jew is taboo in this "democratic" country.

Sir, the African people have been told time and again that they are babies, that they are an inferior race, that they cannot achieve anything worthwhile by themselves or without a white man as their "trustee" or "leader." This insidious suggestion has poisoned their minds and has resulted in a pathological state of mind. Consequently the African has lost or is losing the sterling qualities of self-respect, self-confidence and self-reliance. Even in the political world, it is being suggested that Africans cannot organise themselves or make any progress without white "leaders."

Now I stand for the revolt against this psychological enslavement of my people. I strive for the eradication of this "Ja-Baas" mentality, which for centuries has been systematically and subtlely implanted into the minds of the Africans. Of course this does not at all mean that we reject all political assistance to us by some kind, sympathetic and benevolent white people. "Lending assistance" is to my mind not the same thing as "arrogating to oneself the role of a leader." From then the only assistance which we can accept is that which will help us to consolidate the African tribes into one homogeneous nation.

I understand, Sir, that the "Inkululeko" is the organ of the Communist Party of South Africa. I hope therefore that the "Inkululeko" will not embark on a policy which may culminate in creating or widening a gulf between Communism and African Nationalism in this country; nor exhaust itself in a futile attempt to crush, destroy or extirpate the national consciousness of the African people. It must be remembered that practically every African is a nationalist at heart.

(We are assured by our correspondent that the report which appeared in *Inkululeko* was an accurate and fair comment on Mr. Lembede's speech. There is little to quarrel with what he now says in the above letter, but we are assured that his speech at Orlando was in quite different terms. We are not aware of which organisation Mr. Lembede is referring to as being run by White men or which White people are posing as the leaders of the Africans. In view of the immunity of well known Nazis like Messrs. Pirow, Van Rensburg, Weichardt,[52] etc., we do not think Mr. Lembede need worry about "the peril of internment or deportation." But racialism of the type preached by him at Orlando will do great damage to the true cause of African nationalism. True nationalism lies in love for and pride in one's own people, not the incitement of hatred against others — Editor.)

29. A. M. LEMBEDE, "Fallacy of Non-European Unity Movement," *Bantu World*, 11 August 1945 (also in *Ilanga lase Natal*, 11 August 1945).

A great hullabaloo is being made by advocates of the Unity of all Non-Europeans in South Africa in their struggle against white supremacy or white oppression. This Unity we are told, is to include Africans, Coloureds and Indians.

Before irreparable harm is done to the development and progress of the African people, this fallacious and fantastic theory must be exposed. Unity among the abovementioned classes of Non-Europeans is impossible or extremely difficult of attainment for the following reasons:

(a) Africans are Natives of Africa; they and Africa are one; their relation to Africa is superior to the relations of other sections of the population. This superiority of relation to Africa clearly places the Africans in a position of ascendancy and superiority over other sections of the South African population. Hence it is evidently wrong to place Africans on a footing of equality with other racial groups at present residing in Africa. Africans are fighting for Africa; but other sections are fighting only for their rights to trade and extract as much wealth as possible from Africa.

(b) Another point which renders unity a non-practical proposition is the historical, cultural and religious differences between the above-mentioned classes. The Indians have India as their motherland; they are only here in Africa chiefly as traders. Some of them profess the Mohamedan or the Hindu faith. Even amongst themselves there is no unity on account of their religious differences; otherwise India would have achieved Dominion Status today. Most of the Africans however profess the Christian Faith.

(c) There are three types of Coloureds: firstly there are those who have identified themselves with the Africans, who live with the Africans, and speak African languages and who have thrown in their lot completely with the Africans. These we can tolerate in our society. There is a second class of Coloureds which regards itself as a distinct nation namely Eur-African Nation. The third class of Coloureds consists of those Coloureds who regard themselves as Europeans and look down upon and despise Africans and call them "kaffirs."

(d) It must be remembered also that the first and primary duty of African leaders is to their own people, the Africans. The African leaders are not called upon to lead and organise Coloureds and Indians as some of the bigoted advocates of the Unity movement would have us believe.

(e) The Coloureds and Indians are regarded by Europeans as superior to the Africans and thus deserving of certain rights and privileges which are denied to the Africans, for instance the use of tram cars in Johannesburg, the right to reside and carry on business in certain areas of the town where Africans are prohibited.

But no sane person can deny the fact that there are some common problems confronting Africans and Indians and Coloureds e.g. the right of franchise. The solution of such problems needs the co-operation of all Non-Europeans. But co-operation is different from unity. Africans must be organised as a separate self conscious unit. So likewise must the Coloureds and Indians separately. Then if there is a common problem the leaders of the three sections can come together and take a joint decision as to how the common problem is to be jointly and co-operatively tackled. Then they will return to their respective sections of the population and mobilise the masses for the joint and concerted attack. This is the only sound way which is based on common sense and grim realism. Merely to create a motley horde or a colourless amorphous conglomeration of Africans, Coloureds and Indians will only lead to chaos, to wasted effort and ineffective action.

The call then is: BACK TO COMMON SENSE! BACK FROM JUNGLES OF FANTASIES AND DREAMS! BACK!!!

30. L. B. MEHLOMAKULU, "Non-European Unity Movement," *Bantu World,* 29 September 1945.

IN AN ARTICLE on the above subject published in a recent issue of the "Bantu World," Mr. A. M. Lembede states: "Africans are natives of Africa; they and Africa are one, their relation to Africa is superior to that of other sections of the population. This superiority of relationship clearly places Africans in a position of ascendancy and superiority over other sections; hence it is evidently wrong to place Africans on a footing of equality with other racial groups at present residing in Africa."

On reading this excerpt and the rest of Lembede's letter, repressionists must have felt delighted, for it is a tacit endorsement of their "divide and rule policy," and also an endorsement of the prevailing social inequality among the different racial groups in this country. To claim ascendancy and superiority of Africans over other sections of the South African population simply justifies the whiteman's oppression of Non-Europeans as well as strengthening his claim of rightful possession of this land by reason of his conquest. Besides, to say that historical, cultural and religious differences among non-Europeans render unity a non-practical proposition, is merely to advance a flimsy argument as these differences exist even among Africans themselves. Ample proof can be shown that unity can exist even in diversity. If these differences among non-Europeans render unity impracticable, then Lembede must abandon all hopes of uniting his own people who are no less diverse historically, culturally, religiously and tribally.

The clamour of all right-thinking Africans to-day is for justice which they want extended to all sections of the population, and not the "ascendancy and superiority" of Africans over all others. It is for this cause, justice, that the Non-European Unity Movement strives.[53]

31. M. NDLOVU, "Really, Mr. Lembede," *Ilanga lase Natal,* 15 September 1945.

Recently, Mr. Lembede wrote an article under the heading, 'Man know thyself.' In that article Mr. Lembede would have us believe that certain types of government were created (by whom?) for certain peoples. Communism for the Russians, Democracy for the English etc. Mr. Cele of Durban wrote a very good article in answer to such wrong assertions. But, Mr. Lembede, instead of answering Mr. Cele goes on to write something on the 'Unity Movement' based on his wrong assertions which Mr. Cele corrected, and which corrections Mr. Lembede could not refute. Mr. Lembede is looked upon as a budding young African leader and many young Africans who are too lazy to think for themselves will be misled. Mr. Lembede seems to have a very unhealthy habit of dogmatising. I am not a member of the 'movement' but I know its working and its aims. The fact that I am not a member places me in a better position to see both sides.

In my most humble opinion there are only two reasons that make unity difficult — mind you not impossible. The first is economic, that is, some of the Non-Europeans especially Asiatics, are so rich that they have vested interests which would suffer if unity achieved its aim. The second we will call, for want of a better word, psychological; that is some of the Non-Europeans, especially Coloureds, do not see that the few privileges they get which are denied to others, are nothing but the Government's application of the old slogan 'divide and rule.'

(a) This is rather more amusing than anything else. To the writer it seems the Africans are fighting to drive non-Africans into the sea. The fight, Sir, is for a right for everyone to live. (All these races who are in the Union have come to stay, figuratively and literally, and we have to live with them willy nilly). Indians have as much a right to live here as negroes have in the U.S.A. According to the writer's theory of 'superiority' only Red Indians have a right to fight for America; all the others are fighting for trading rights. We leave it to you, dear reader.

(b) The Unity movement is not a cultural or religious body, it's a political body whose aim is to fight against oppression based on colour. The writer cannot sanely deny the fact that if all the laws applied to Africans were applied to other non-Europeans unity would not only be practicable but inevitable, despite the historical, cultural, and religious differences.

(c) The writer here agrees with us that the only difficulty is presented by the inequality of oppression and the failure of some Indians and Coloureds to see through the covering.

(d) Who said Africans must leave their people and work for the liberation of Indians and Coloureds? I am afraid the writer shows an unhealthy ignorance of the working of the movement.

If the writer's argument that there are fundamental differences among these races which make unity impossible were carried to its logical conclusion, it would mean that even among Africans themselves there can be no unity because the tribes have different backgrounds, customs etc. So that even a national body like Congress is, in the writer's language (God, what language!) composed of 'a motley horde or a colourless amorphous conglomeration of Basutos, Xosas, Zulus etcs.'

32. A. M. LEMBEDE, "African Trade Unions," n.d., unpublished.[54]

As things are today, Africans as employees in European Industrial areas have to fight for adequate wages improved conditions of employment and the right to do and be employed in any skilled jobs. The lack of these three elementary human rights is at the root of the alarming physical and moral deterioration of the African urban society. Unless the Africans desperate fight is crowned with success the above mentioned deterioration will certainly and rapidly culminate in a national disaster or calamity. Among Africans in urban areas death rate is alarmingly high especially child mortality. The moral tone of society is on the downward grade. The excessive use of alcohol and hooliganism are prevalent. All this is due to the economic exploitation of the African by white capitalists and oppression of Africans as a black race.

It becomes imperatively necessary therefore that African workers organise themselves and fight furiously and resolutely for an adequate wage which will enable them to live decently with their wives and children. Now an African family of say four (father mother and two kiddies) cannot in my opinion live decently on a wage of less than £9 a month. But today there are families of six or seven who are compelled to live on a wage of £2 or £4 a month or less. It is a shame!

It is thus crystal clear that the struggle of African Trade Unions is indissolubly bound up with the African National Struggle for existence and survival in an industrial era. Strictly speaking it is the right to live in the land of their birth. Hence it is an illusion of demented political demagogues to imagine that African workers as such can achieve their emancipation and reach their goal of being recognised by the government on the same footing as Europeans Trade Unions while the rest of the African nation is still in chains and bondage of segregation oppression and colour discrimination.

It is appropriate here to dismiss a certain fallacious doctrine which is being propounded and disseminated by some trade unionists — especially some white men and other foreigners — under the influence of foreign ideologies and under the meaningless slogan or cry of "Workers of South Africa Unite" thereby urging all workers — African, Indian, coloured and European — to unite and overthrow the capitalist class.

The emptiness or bankruptcy of the above mentioned cry or slogan becomes self-evident when one observes that Africans are not primarily oppressed as workers but are oppressed on the ground of colour or race. The Union Colour Bar Act,[55] the Industrial Conciliation Act,[56] the Urban Areas Act, the Masters and Servants Act[57] etc are designed to "keep the Native in his place."

Moreover, the European coloured and Indian workers are so solicitous and anxious about safe guarding the precious rights they now enjoy of being employed as skilled workers and artisans that they are reluctant or strongly opposed to opening the door to competition with numerically stronger Africans. Generally speaking it is these non-African workers who determinedly stand in the way of success and recognition of African Trade Unions.

Supposing a labour government came into power today, would the African trade unions be recognised tomorrow? Not at all. Remember there is still something like "white supremacy" to be maintained at all cost in South Africa and about which all white people are agreed.

Again it is well known that Indians and Coloureds are regarded by the Europeans as superior to Africans and thus deserving certain privileges denied to Africans — thus rendering harmony very difficult if not impossible.

We should not forget also that even before the rise of capitalism in South Africa, that is during the days of the boer republics, it was constitutionally laid down that "Daar sal geen gelykstelling tussen blankes en kaffers wees nie, of in die kerk of in die Stadt." ["There shall be no equality between whites and blacks in church and state."]

To conclude my argument I may point out that there are some few wealthy Africans with bank balances running to five figures — capitalists in the usual sense of the word. But are these admitted into the ranks and society of white capitalists? May they attend same cinemas, concerts etc. together with their white prototypes? Why? Colour and race.

Today African trade unions present a monstrous pitiful bizarre spectacle; they have degenerated into a play ground or battlefield — I do not know which is which — for foreign ideologies of the so called "white Native leaders." African trade union leaders have become mere puppets in the hands of foreigners or foreign agents.

If therefore we are not to violate the canons of common sense we must unequivocally and emphatically state that African Trade Unions should be permeated and galvanised into a dynamic militant national trade union movement — an important wing of the Africanistic movement aiming at national liberation and racial survival. I am of the opinion that African farm workers on European farms should be organised into a powerful trade union. If we adopt this course the triumph, success and victory of the African Trade Unions may be a *fait accompli* within our lifetime or at least earlier than we can imagine.

Let us get rid of hallucinations; let us tackle the problem of African Trade Unions with grim realism and in the light of stern reality.

33. A. M. LEMBEDE, "The I.C.U. and the A.N.C.," *Ilanga lase Natal*, 26 October 1946.

RUMOUR IS widespread that the I.C.U.[58] may stage a dramatic comeback. Such a move would be whole-heartedly welcomed by Africans who are hectically seeking for dynamic leadership; for inspite of its numerous faults, the I.C.U. had many exquisite virtues two of which are: its dynamic leadership and its purely Africanistic orientation. The I.C.U. was not a radio-controlled robot of some countries over the seas. It was an indigenous movement similar to the A.N.C.

A note of warning and caution must however be sounded. The I.C.U. leaders who may be labouring to revive the I.C.U. must keep in mind that times and circumstances have fundamentally changed. From 1926 to 1946 is a long way. History is moving forward inexorably by leaps and bounds. The I.C.U. cannot be revived in its old spirit. Oh no! but on a higher plane of clarity of vision and a saner sense of balance and responsibility.

When the I.C.U. was at the crest of its highest tide, the A.N.C. was at its lowest ebb. Between the two organisations there deplorably prevailed a spirit of mutual suspicion, unfriendliness and animosity. There was no rapprochement or co-operation. Both organisations failed to produce a leader that could transcend petty personal jealousies and hatreds and galvanize the two organisations into one or co-ordinate them on a higher rational basis. The result was that the I.C.U. totally eclipsed the A.N.C. and raged like wild veld fire throughout South Africa — which veld fire gradually consumed itself and fizzled out at the same period the A.N.C. became dormant and semi-defunct.

The failure of co-operation and co-ordination between the I.C.U. and the A.N.C. was a tragedy of the grimmest character. The clock of our progress towards national emancipation was thereby put back indefinitely. Can we allow such a fatal error to be repeated today?

The African workers have to be organised into a single solid labour organisation which must be an essential wing of the national movement. It is a gross fallacy to imagine that the struggle of the African worker is separable or apart from the whole national struggle of the African people for liberation. To my mind it is the task of a movement like the I.C.U. to wage the economic and industrial warfare while the political aspect thereof is entrusted to the hands of the A.N.C. The struggle is one but only aspects differ. Thus the intrinsic nature of the struggle demands one national movement with the I.C.U. and A.N.C. aspects thereof. Both I.C.U. and A.N.C. should be complementary to each other. An A.N.C. without a workers organisation (like the I.C.U.) is a motionless cripple and the I.C.U. without the A.N.C. is a ghost-like skeleton.

Today the African Trade Unions are in a deplorable state, a sad plight. They are being torn and tossed about by foreigners and foreign ideologies. If African trade unions are not rescued as early as possible, Africans will be overcome by a sense of frustration and lose confidence in the Trade Union movement. What a calamity! With the poet we may thus say: "I.C.U. thou shouldst be living at this hour, Africa has need of thee."[59]

The A.N.C. is faced with two inescapable alternatives — and it must adopt one or other if it is to survive — either to launch out its own militant workers' organisation or to assist with all its might, in the revival of the I.C.U. in the new spirit of Africanism — the outlook of the African continent. The last alternative appears to me to be within the limits of immediate possibility and highly commendable.

Let us all (I.C.U. & A.N.C.) outgrow our petty personal jealousies and the consuming lust for high positions; let us extricate ourselves from the shackles of narrow and parochial views of one another and of our momentous struggle; let us fix our gaze on the wider and ever receding horizons. Africa must be free; Africa must take her honourable and rightful place amongst the nations of the world.

34. T. NDLANGAMADLA, "A Challenge to Mr. A. M. Lembede," *Ilanga lase Natal,* 23 November 1946.

THE *Ilanga* of the 19/10/46 was worth reading with its columns full of interesting articles dealing with our national problems.

One of the notable articles was that drawn by the great African thinker and planner Mr. Lembede, a carefully considered article reviewing the past and never to return history of the A.N.C. as compared with that of the I.C.U.

Perhaps we all know that the African National Congress is the national and foremost political organisation of the African peoples.

I need not comment on the I.C.U. and its followers; one remarkable factor of the I.C.U. was its stupid unfounded belief in force instead of right.

Let us now consider Mr. Lembede's article in which he proposes:

(1) The revival of the I.C.U.

(2) Two African political armies (A.N.C. and I.C.U.) to fight for African Liberation.

(3) Believes that an A.N.C. without or not backed by the I.C.U. is a skeleton organisation.

It is clear that Mr. Lembede before taking his pen, remembered the "Look before you leap" talk; although he succeeded to a considerable extent in convincing our well known "Yes Men" and also the ambitious former I.C.U. leaders, he failed out-right to convince the seasoned veterans of our politics.

These seasoned veterans of our advocated unity will even at "pistol point" oppose the Lembede idea. Does Mr. Lembede see any possibility of two bulls agreeing in one kraal?

Does he believe that the I.C.U. can work on good terms with the African National Congress?

Does he mean that he has no confidence in the A.N.C. as an organisation capable of solving African affairs?

In my opinion the Lembede idea is not based on any fundamental facts or proofs; it only disqualifies the Lembedes.

It may be the aim of Mr. Lembede to witness a political war in the African Liberation movement.

35. A. M. LEMBEDE, "Mr. Msimang Answered," *Ilanga lase Natal,* 19 July 1947.

IN YOUR ISSUE of a few weeks ago you published a letter [28 June 1947] by Mr. Selby Msimang,[60] Secretary A.N.C. (Natal) in which, Mr. Msimang appealed to the African people in the Union not to reject in toto the recent General Smuts proposals but to consider them and accept what is good; and he further makes a lot of hullabaloo about the new powers of the N.R.C. to govern and administer the Native Reserves especially if General Smuts would provide facilities for Africans to be trained as artisans, technicians and skilled labourers.

Now the argument that General Smuts' proposals be carefully considered and what is good in them be accepted is not new. The same argument was used "successfully" during the great historic 1936 sell-out to the extreme delight and satisfaction of General Hertzog — but with disastrous results to the African people. There will be no more 1936![61]

In the Reserves the Government is growing unpopular, for, instead of providing more land is calling upon Africans to limit their stock. This unpleasant task, it is now intended to delegate to Africans themselves. In other words the N.R.C. will be made a cat's paw. I also visualise a terrible friction between the N.R.C. and the African Chiefs in the Reserves whose power, influence and prestige will be seriously threatened by the N.R.C.'s administration of Reserves.

Mr. Msimang as a veteran and experienced politician should realise that the Government will never make the Reserves very attractive and comfortable to live in because that would stop influx of cheap African labourers into European urban areas. Where will the Chamber of Mines,[62] for instance, recruit its huge army of cheap African mine workers?

As to the training of skilled African workers, there can be no large-scale training of Africans as technicians, engineers, magistrates, etc. until Colour Bar laws are scrapped from the statute book of the Union. Until and unless this is done, there will always be "white bosses" and "African boys" even in the Reserves, just as in African education you have white inspectors and African boys called supervisors.

No, Mr. Msimang, be clear-minded, we don't want a bone to chew. We want meat to eat. We are not dogs.

Anton Lembede's primary school class, Umbumbulu, 1927. Anton is tenth from the left on the bottom row. His brother, Nicholas, is fifth from the left and Bernadette Sibeko eighth from the left on the bottom row.

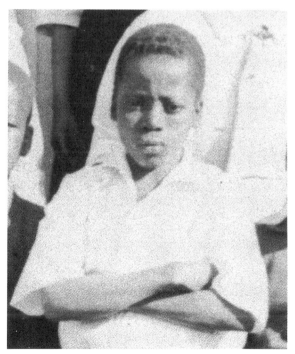

Inset of Anton Lembede, age 13.

Sister Bernadette Sibeko, Assisi Convent, Port Shepstone, 1992.

Anton Lembede and A. P. Mda at a Catholic teachers' conference, late 1930s.

A. P. Mda, Mafeteng, Lesotho, 1986.

Anton Lembede, mid-1940s.

Anton Lembede, mid-1940s.

Anton Lembede and A. P. Mda at Mda's graduation ceremony, 26 July 1947.

A. P. Mda and Anton Lembede at Mda's graduation ceremony,
26 July 1947.

Lembede's grave, Croesus Cemetery, Johannesburg.

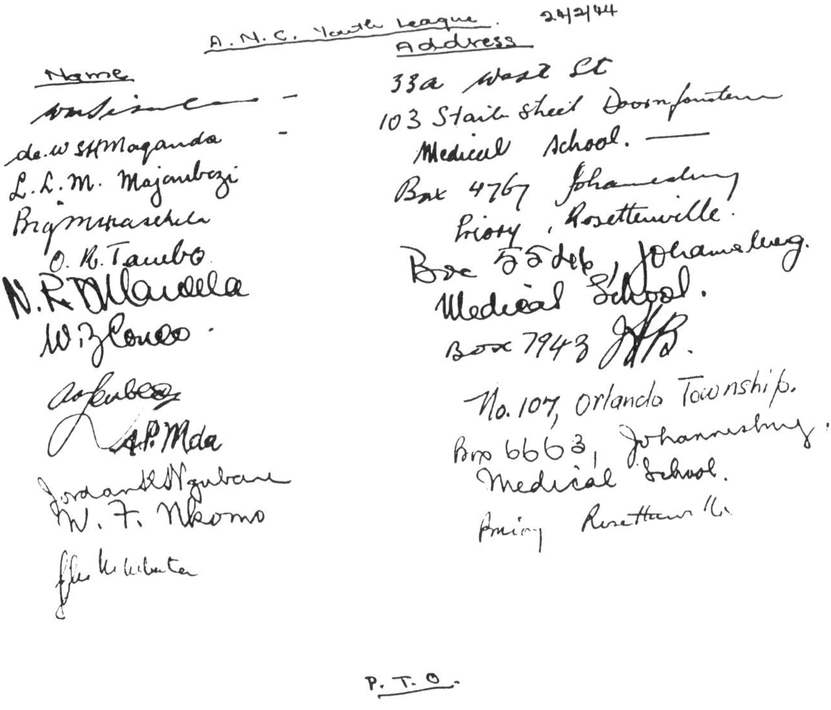

A. N. C. Youth League. 24/2/44

Name   Address

[signatures, handwritten, illegible]
de.W SH Maganda   33a West St
L.L.M. Majombozi   103 Stair Street Doornfontein
Big mxasekela   Medical School. —
O. R. Tambo   Box 4767 Johannesburg
N.R. Dlandela   Priory, Rosettenville.
W Z Conco   Box 55 del, Johannesburg.
[signature]   Medical School.
A.P. Mda   Box 7943 JHB.
Jordan K Ngubane   No. 107, Orlando Township.
W. F. Nkomo   Box 6663, Johannesburg.
[signature]   Medical School.
                         Priory Rosettenville.

P. T. O.

Attendance sheet for ANC Youth League meeting, 24 February 1944. The names (from top to bottom) are: Walter Sisulu, W. S. Maganda, L. L. M. Majombozi, Big P. T. O. Masekela, Oliver Tambo, Nelson Mandela, W. Z. Conco, Anton Lembede, A. P. Mda, Jordan Ngubane, W. F. Nkomo, and Congress Mbata.

CULTURAL
ACTIVITIES

36. "MR. LEMBEDE'S RECEPTION," *Inkundla ya Bantu,* August (Second Fortnight, 1946).

A GOOD and representative crowd attended the reception to celebrate the academic achievement of Mr. A. M. Lembede M.A., LL.B at the B.M.S.C. on Friday 26th July 1946. The "function" was organised by the African National Congress Youth League of which Mr. Lembede is a President. Dr. J. M. Nhlapo[63] was in the chair, and Dr. A. B. Xuma,[64] Mr. W. F. Nkomo, B.Sc. (a medical student) and Mr. A. P. Mda paid tribute to Mr. Lembede in eloquent speeches which were loudly cheered.

Opening the reception Dr. Nhlapo who now and then regaled the house from his inexhaustible fund of humour paid a powerful and flowing tribute to Mr. Lembede's exceptional and unprecedented achievement.

Mr. A. P. Mda said that Mr. Lembede had scored success in the realm of philosophy which curiously enough had been considered a special preserve for the whites. His success was a clarion call to the rising generation to rise and fight for freedom for a people that can produce the Lembedes is a people worthy of the rich heritage of freedom. He then solemnly advised Mr. Lembede to remain humble in success and not to lose the "common touch."

Dr. A. B. Xuma has a knack of saying wise things on occasions like these. He was in his best element. He said that many of us engage in idle criticism and thus become blind to see the greater things of life. "Many of us look for green pastures elsewhere" and fail to see the possibilities of progress at the tips of our very toes. He then related Booker T. Washington's famous story, ending in the well-known "Cast the bucket where you are!"[65] Opportunity had to be seized by the fore lock, he said, and it was gratifying to note that Mr. Lembede had learnt this fact not theoretically but in practice. The rise of Mr. Lembede should be an inspiration to all; by his rise he had established a milestone in our history. "We must learn to worship achievement and above all to emulate achievement" he concluded. He then shook hands with Mr. Lembede amid cheers.

In paying tribute to Mr. Lembede, Mr. W. Nkomo said that Lembede had risen from humble beginnings to M.A. Already he had distinguished himself as a lawyer, and as one who was prepared to serve his people. He said that Lembede's proficiency in languages like Afrikaans was an example and an inspiration to Transvaal youth.

Mr. A. M. Lembede replied in a memorable speech. He took the Platonic view for his definition of philosophy, and said that the function of a philosopher was to be a spectator for "all time and existence." Philosophy, he said, sees the Universe as a whole. He also showed that philosophy was practical or at least that some of its conclusions could be translated into practice. Hegel taught that the spirit was superior to matter and he developed his theory of dialectics. Karl Marx inverted this and said that matter was superior to the spirit, that is to say, he took a materialistic view. But Karl Marx retained the dialectical theory of Hegel. Marxism is the dominant outlook of Soviet Russia. Mr. Lembede said that Nazi philosophy was based on "Darwinism" i.e. survival of the "fittest" while the utilitarian outlook dominated British thinking for a number of decades. He also brought in the American system of thought based on pragmatism.

When he climbed down from these heights to a discourse on African Nationalism he made a deep impression on the house. Nationalism, he said, was a new conception, a new bond which should bind the tribes into a single whole. Mr. Lembede rejected internationalism as a stage before nationalism. A truly international society is not possible whilst the overwhelming majority of the peoples of the earth are backward. He summarily dismissed the claims of pseudo internationalist propagandists.

Mr. Lembede also made it clear that African Nationalism is not in substance against other Non-European groups. African Nationalism is definitely against foreign domination of any description and from whatever quarter it comes. It visualises the rise and emergence of Black Africa as a world power. It believes in the leadership of Africa by Africans and rejects white leadership.

Mr. Lembede was given a great ovation.

Apologies were received from Mrs. Madie Hall Xuma,[66] Rev. H. Mpitso, Mr. J. B. Marks, Mr. T. Ntwasa[67] (a Johannesburg Attorney) and from Dr. P. ka I. Seme.[68] Music was rendered by the "Manhattan Stars" and the "Philharmonic Choral Society," whilst the Merry Blackbirds Orchestra played for the dance.

37. A. P. MDA, "Here and There," *Um-Afrika,* 14 September 1946.

A MARATHON DEBATE. One of the biggest and most fiercely-contested debates ever held in Johannesburg, was staged at the Bantu Men's Social Centre[69] early in August. The B.M.S.C. represented by Messrs. A. M. Lembede, V. V. T. Mbobo[70] and A. P. Mda, was ranged against Port Elizabeth represented by O. G. Socenywa, B. G. Ximya, and W. F. Hermans, and the topic was: "Resolved, that Communism is better than Democracy." We took the negative and Port Elizabeth took the affirmative. Mr. Socenywa, ably supported by the other speakers put up the case in support of the Soviet system of "collective farming," planned Socialist economy and the elimination (liquidation) of exploitation of "man by man," unemployment and social insecurity. When Mr. Socenywa (P. E.) stood up to summarise the case for Port Elizabeth, he broke out into passionate outbursts of gripping oratory, in the course of which he brought down the packed hall, whilst administering savage punishment on his opponents.

Mr. Lembede and Mr. Mbobo, on our side, were concerned with the presentation of facts in favour of British and American democracy. Mr. Lembede was cheered again and again, when he argued that under democracy there was the "rule of law," and the recognition of the dignity of human personality, and that political power was enthroned in the enfranchised masses of the people. He was forcefully and eloquently supported by Mr. V. V. T. Mbobo, B.A., B. Econ., who approached the subject from the economic standpoint. The "offensive" was reserved for Mr. A. P. Mda, who had to demolish the opposition's defences. With devastating logic and seething satire, Mr. A. P. Mda rained blow upon blow upon the opposition. He vehemently denounced Soviet Russia as a vast bureaucracy with supreme and unlimited power vested in the 13 members of the "politburo," and exposed the vaunted "dictatorship of the proletariat" as the dictatorship of the Communist Party, with the General Secretary of the Supreme Soviet as the virtual tyrant, bully and despot. He denounced the State Capitalism practised in Russia, and said that a state where there is no technique of change except by bloody revolution cannot, in the long run, be a guarantor of individual freedom, development and self-expression. Messrs. James Mdatyulwa[71] and R. Peteni,[72] B.A., gave a reasoned judgment, awarding 251 points to the B.M.S.C. as against 221 to the Port Elizabeth Club. Thus Johannesburg upheld its reputation by giving the Cape a trouncing. The standard of the debate was very high. Port Elizabeth put up a "terrific" fight.

A big reception in Honour of Lembede. During the third week of July, the "Congress Youth League," organised a well-patronised and well-attended reception in honour of A. M. Lembede, Esq., M.A. LL.B., at the B.M.S.C. Very able and instructive speeches were delivered on the occasion by Dr. J. M. Nhlapho [sic], B.A., Ph.D., who presided; Dr. A. B. Xuma, President General of Congress; W. F. Nkomo, B.A., B.Sc., a medical student, and Mr. A. P. Mda who spoke on behalf of the "National Executive of Youth League." Music was rendered by the "Manhattan Stars" and the "Orlando Philharmonic Choir"; the "Merry Black Birds Band" played for the ball.

Mr. A. M. Lembede is now a fully-fledged lawyer. He is in partnership with Dr. P. I. Seme, who has however moved to Edendale in the Pietermaritzburg district. Mr. A. M. Lembede's office is at Nos. 2-3 Rosenburg Arcade, 58 Market Street, Johannesburg.

38. A. M. LEMBEDE, Book Review of *Nje-Nempela* by B. Wallet Vilakazi, *Teachers' Quarterly Review,* I, 2 (September 1946), 8-10.

OUR CHECKERED South African History furnishes a novelist with ample and abundant material for a novel. This exquisite material has not — I regret to say — been fully exploited by our Bantu writers; of course some writers have availed themselves of this material for various purposes, as witness, Dlomo's [sic] "U Dingane," Mofolo's "Chaka," Dube's "U Jeqe," etc.[73]

The above mentioned book by Mr. Vilakazi[74] is a historical novel. The events take place in and about 1906 in Natal; that was during Bambatha's bloody rebellion[75] against the Natal Government on the ground of the imposing of poll tax on Africans in Natal.

A kraal youth, Malambule, left his home at Inkandhla near Tugela River and went to work in the Gold Mines of Barberton (Transvaal) where he came into contact with a new mode of life — European civilisation with its attendant moral dissoluteness and corruption — which was entirely different from kraal life. After working there for several years he decided to return to his father's kraal. The journey of several days was accomplished on foot. On a certain day at sunset, while he was on his way home, Malambule called on a kraal near the way at a place called Dumbe and asked for accomodation for the night. This kraal belonged to one Nomona Nkominophondo, and Malambule was cordially welcomed there. Here he met one of the daughters of Nkominophondo (who was a polygamist). Her name was Nomcebo. At first sight she inwardly fell in love with Malambule but when he later made formal advances she proudly and defiantly replied, "WENA UNGUBANI — NJE — NEMPELA"; "What are you at all?" Hence the title of this book. Having fallen sick, the hero of the story was nursed for several days by the mother of Nomcebo. Among those Malambule met at this kraal were Zazini, brother to Nomcebo, and a certain Maphulane, sort of a clown, skilled in magic and drugs (reminding us of Shakespearean clowns). Having proposed to Nomcebo with partial success and having given a fine shawl to her mother as a token of gratitude, Malambule departed and continued his long tedious journey homewards. Before leaving, however, he informed Maphulane that he would return one day to fetch Nomcebo and marry her.

The country was in a turbulent state. Bambatha had refused to pay poll tax and defied the Government at Greytown. Many Chiefs staunchly supported him but there were also many Quislings. One Chakiyane was leader of a terrorist organisation whose aim was to exterminate all quislings ruthlessly, and thus facilitate the mobilization of all warriors against the white government and assure victory in battle without danger of being stabbed in the back.

When Malambule reached home he immediately sent a group of young men including his brothers, to go and fetch Nomcebo, who, unknown to Malambule (with Bembesile, her jealous half-sister) had already been coerced to go and marry the son of a certain Chief Sishishili. When they reached the kraal of Nkominophondo, these envoys of Malambule were informed of this terrible news. They decided to trace Nomcebo and abduct her. Maphulane accompanied them. They succeeded in abducting Nomcebo at midnight. Shortly after this, the Chief's kraal was suddenly and unexpectedly stormed by the terrorist group — for Chief Sishishili was suspected of being a quisling — and the inmates of the kraal together with visitors, in the midst of their wedding festivities were practically wiped out with a ruthless iron hand. Nomcebo escaped, joined Malambule's messengers and proceeded with them to the home of her lover.

In the meantime Malambule had been recruited into the black army but when he was sent by his Commandant to accompany a band of warriors whose task it was to rob and plunder a certain shop and kill the owner (at Mpanza), he deserted and went over to the white men at Greytown where he was employed as a wagon driver.

The zero hour struck. White met Black in battle. The blacks were unable to hold their own in face of superior arms and weapons. Bambatha was killed. Dinizulu was suspected of conspiracy partly on the grounds of some secret information treacherously given to Europeans at Greytown by Bambatha's wife. He was arrested and brought to trial as an accomplice and instigator. Malambule attended the trial and gave evidence — to confirm his own father's evidence — for the crown. Dinizulu was found guilty.

Thereafter Malambule and his father returned home where Nomcebo was already waiting. Malambule's happiness at seeing her was boundless. His cup of joy overflowed. Nomcebo too was full of mirth to see her lover and prospective husband; but on that very day Malambule's father died. After the funeral Malambule feared that since he was a traitor, people might make an attempt on his life, so he took Nomcebo and fled to the white man's land, accompanied by Maphulane and others. Here the story ends.

The time and circumstances which form the background of this story are excellent and judiciously selected by the Author.

The mastery and manipulation of language leaves very little to be desired. The prose style is simple, straightforward, descriptive and narrative. It is rather heavy and solid although here and there it rises

to some lyrical heights; e.g. Page 14; "Waphuma uMalambule wayi-
buka lenyanga, phansi kwayo kude, empumalanga wabona iziqongo
zoBombo, zithe thushu, thushu thushu ziphakeme phezulu ezulwini,"
["Malambule went outside, he looked at the moon, and way below it
on the eastern horizon, he saw the crest of the mountain range rising
up to the sky above."] — and (Page 113) — "Izulu phandhle lalisile
lilihle izinkanyezi zonke zichithekile emkhathini wezulu ziqhweba
okuemhlabeni ngokucwazimula kwazo." ["The sky outside was clear,
the stars were scattered across the entire sky, beckoning the earth
with their luster."]

   The writer has at his disposal a tremendous wealth of descriptive
verbs such as chwabaza, nqekulisana, gswaneka, qundeka, vaveka, xo-
bisa etc., and such descriptive words as jeqe! yatho! zu! etc. His language is also enriched and embellished by the use of proverbs — e.g.
"Induku enhle egawula ezizweni" ["a beautiful stick (kierie) is cut
from trees from afar."]; "Indoda kayifeli ecansini, ifela ezibini" ["a
man does not die on his sleeping mat but wherever he falls."] etc.

   By the dexterous employment of Zulu war songs, and the praises,
(izibongo) of the warriors and heroes the writer attempts to describe
and portray historical events and circumstances, and thus re-create
the atmosphere of the times; also the dialogue form of conversation
heightens the realistic setting thereof.

   The writer succeeds in captivating the interest of the reader and in
keeping his sense of expectation in suspense till the end. The writer
also fairly well demonstrates the inevitable clash of cultures — namely,
the primitive Bantu and the advanced European.

   There are however, some weaknesses in the story. Firstly, the writer
often fails to give a full and satisfactory description. Some events and
episodes are dismissed with a few words or cursorily dealt with. In this
way the background of the story suffers and consequently the story itself, for the story should be cast in a clear relief of its background —
e.g., the formalities of "ukucela intombi"[76] when Sishishili's men come
to "cela" Nomcebo and Bembesile; formalities and details of a typical
Zulu wedding, at Sishishili's kraal, — the vivid picture of the great
battle between Bambatha's forces and the European soldiers, — proper
and realistic description of the trial of Chief Dinizulu at Greytown,

death of Malambule's father, etc. An historical novel should, in my opinion, give us an insight into, or knowledge of, the social practises, institutions and conditions of the times. The impression I have is that the story was pieced together rather too quickly. I say this on the authority of some European Novels I have read — e.g., Thackeray's "Vanity Fair," and several Afrikaans Novels such as "Die Vreemdeling," "Die Hugenotebloed," etc.[77]

Again, the writer selects for his hero, or one of the heroes of his book, a traitor, a quisling — Malambule — a man who deserts his own people at a critical moment when they are facing a formidably powerful enemy; and who at the Court Trial, gives evidence against his own Paramount Chief Dinizulu. It is quite true there might have been such cowardly characters, but to my mind, it is highly undesirable to give them publicity or emphasis. This may sew [sic] the seed of a defeatist mentality or an inferiority complex in the minds of our children. As Plato says in the "Republic" — "in training youth, we should never tell them of the disgraceful and dishonourable deeds of their ancestors." So likewise, we should not tell our children that we were routed, humiliated and cowed by white people, we should merely tell them that in the face of superior forces and weapons, we were compelled to lay down arms — but our National Spirit is invincible, unconquerable, and hence we shall relentlessly continue the fierce struggle by acquiring and using the new weapons of Western Culture and Civilisation.

However the stress laid on the writer's failure to disapprove strongly of and condemn the scandalous act of Bambatha's wife who treacherously divulged — although of course, with a quasi-innocent intention of exonerating her husband — some facts which led to the arrest of Chief Dinizulu in connection with the rebellion, is deplorable. As a rule, our African women are of a noble and heroic mould, and that is what should be stressed. One also wonders how a girl of such noble and sterling character as Nomcebo was, could willingly and gladly marry Malambule, a National traitor, and without "lobolo" at that. The motto of a National hero should be "My people, right or wrong."

The book also contains some self-contradiction; while in the introduction the writer tells us that he is setting out to show the bravery, courage and heroism of our ancestors, the story tends to prove the diametric opposite.

In conclusion, coming now to the assessment of the literary merits and value of the writer's present work, I hold that the writer did not top or exceed the highest notch — though the material at his disposal and the plan and conception of the present work allowed it — which he registered with his previous novel, — NOMA NINI.[78]

39. A. M. LEMBEDE, "An African Academy of Sciences," *Inkundla ya Bantu,* August 1947.

IN A SUB-EDITORIAL of the "INKUNDLA" of a few weeks ago the Editor pleaded very strongly for the formation of some academy for the advancement of Bantu Art and Literature.

This grand suggestion ought to receive a country-wide approval and support and it should be translated into action without any further waste of time.

Almost all civilised or progressive nations have such academies. Even in our country such organisations exist amongst the whites e.g. Die Skrywerkring, Die Akademie vir Wetenskap en Kuns, The Society for the Advancement of Science etc.[79] The phenomenal growth of the Afrikaans language and literature can, to a very great extent be ascribed to the "akademie." Systematisation of organisation is the basis of progress in all spheres of life.

We need science to assist us in our present stage of transition and we shall need it more increasingly thereafter. To the question: What knowledge is of most value — the uniform reply is: science. We need science in our agriculture, our diet, our homes, for our health, in the upbringing of our children, in the organisation of our economic enterprises and in all departments of our material struggle and existence. It is science that will help us to adapt ourselves to the Western standards of life and to dispel the fogs of ignorance and superstition. Why can't we establish a society for the advancement of science amon[g]st

Africans, to propagate simply scientific knowledge preferably in vernacular, amongst the African masses? Where are our B.Sc's? Where are our laymen interested in science and the problems of science?

Our Art (including literature) can also receive a great impetus and fillip, from a cultural society or academy of art. Artists in different categories of art such as sculpture, painting, drawing, music, literature would tremendously be encouraged by exchange of ideas amongst themselves and competition for annual prizes. Art is indispensable to a nation in the process of being born. We need artists to interpret to us and to the world our glorious past, our misery, suffering and tribulation of the present time, our hopes, aspirations and our divine destiny and our great future; to inspire us with the message that there is hope for our race and that we ought therefore to draw plans and lay foundations for a longer future than we can imagine by struggling for national freedom so as to save our race from imminent extinction or extermination. In short we need African Artists to interpret the spirit of Africa.

I am here confining myself to the utilitarian or pragmatic value of science and art. Space will not allow me to deal with the study of science or art for its own sake.

Now the question is how to proceed in order to found such an academy. I do not think we should start with a big conference at Bloemfontein as the editor of the Inkundla suggests. In my opinion a few protagonists of this project should meet say, in Durban to form a small nucleus committee to draw a comprehensive plan or manifesto, embodying both science and art which will be the basis of the objectives, scope of activities, programme and policy, of the academy. It will then be the primary duty of this committee to propagate and disseminate these things and contact all African scientists and artists as well as laymen, who are interested in science or are lovers of art — appealing to them to join or support the proposed academy. The committee must also find funds in order to organise and direct this large scale propaganda. Thereafter a national conference can be convened. To my mind, this conference should mark the end of the first phase of the whole project and at the same time the beginning of the second phase — namely the consolidation of the academy and extension of its work to the general masses, for, the principal and ultimate aim of the academy should be to educate the masses in the practical application of science and the spiritually elevating appreciation of art.

40. A. M. LEMBEDE, "Congratulations to the Child — 8 Years Old," *Inkundla ya Bantu,* 17 May 1945.

"THE WHOLE TECHNIQUE of propaganda has undergone revolutionary changes in recent years with the remarkable progress of its main agencies — the press, the films and broadcasting. The increase of education has played into the hands of propaganda; and political changes have widened the field for experiment." — A. J. Mackenzie (*Propaganda Boom*).[80]

When the Editor of the "Inkundla ya Bantu" approached and requested me to say something on the occasion of the celebration of the 8th birthday of the "Inkundla ya Bantu,"[81] I felt myself unequal to the task, but we may never say "no" to the call to serve the National cause.

The value of the press in educating and enlightening the masses, in shaping and moulding public opinion, cannot be overestimated. According to Dicey (Law of the Constitution),[82] the freedom of the press (which is part of freedom of speech and discussion) is so important that in several states of Europe it is specifically safeguarded in the constitutions of those states.

Although Hitler says that great historical movements have owed their success to the spoken word, yet no one can doubt the historical role played by such books as the Bible, the Koran, Plato's "Republic," the "Wealth of Nations," "Origin of Species," "Das Kapital," etc. and by such newspapers as "Pravda," "Volkischer Beobachter," "London Times," etc., and by numerous periodicals.

In South Africa, and as far as Africans are concerned, the Press is confronted with two formidable difficulties. Firstly, the immense illiteracy of the African masses. It is said that only about 20 per cent can read and write. Secondly, even among those few literate and educated, there prevails that apathy or lack of that craving or desire for reading which Afrikaners call "lecalus" [leeslus]. Very few Africans care to read their newspapers intelligently.

Evidently the preliminary task of the African Press is twofold: (a) to agitate for the spread of general education among the masses; (b) to write and publish such interesting articles as will awaken and sharpen the appetite for reading among the masses. A newspaper that will strive for this will be rendering an immortal service to our race. The "Inkundla ya Bantu" has undoubtedly embarked on this gigantic campaign. If space allowed me I could quote copiously from several issues of the "Inkundla ya Bantu."

Last year also — if I may remind the reader — the "Inkundla ya Bantu" contributed substantially towards combating and stamping out the discussion or petty quarrel or vendetta between the then existing two Congress factions in Natal.[83]

"Inkundla ya Bantu" is a purely African paper — established by Africans, run by Africans and for Africans. It is a living tribute to the organising administrative, journalistic and editorial genius of the African race.

May the "Inkundla ya Bantu" continue — without swerving or wavering — in building the African nation and helping the nation to march triumphantly forward and occupy its rightful and honourable place among the nations of the world.

In conclusion may I again express my felicitation to the "Inkundla ya Bantu" on its 8th birthday with the wish and hope that the "Inkundla ya Bantu" may soon become a weekly paper or even a daily.[84] If not, why not?

TRIBUTES TO
LEMBEDE
AFTER HIS
DEATH

41. WALTER NHLAPO, "He Sang and Soared Away," *Barlow's Weekly*, 16 August 1947.

Walter Nhlapo (d. 1967) was a journalist employed by Umteteli wa Bantu *and a frequent contributor and letter writer to newspapers and magazines. He was also a talent scout for the Gallo recording company.*

I BELIEVE some Europeans were surprised when they read the news item headlined "Death of a Noted African Lawyer." They were surprised because they had not heard of a Bantu lawyer before.

Those who had known his dynamic personality on the political, educational and legal platforms must have been shocked by his early and untimely death.

He was a fine example of a self-made man. He burned the midnight oil from University Junior Certificate to M.A., LL.B. Only a year ago he received his Master of Arts degree by presenting the thesis: "The Conception of God As Propounded By Great Philosophers From The Time of Descartes To The Present Day."

Africans deeply mourn his departure. He passed in the prime of life, when his acts and deeds were showing a Midas touch. In the words of a wiser man: "It is not the tragedy of death that we lament, but the tragedy of life." We feel that Death has been unkind. It nipped the bud in its first spring. Darkness descended at sun-rise.

A LINGUIST

He was a thinker. He was a brilliant scholar, who was thrilled by the philosophic writings of Hegel, Spinoza, Socrates and Aristotle. Goethe's poetry in the German language was his inspiration. The writings of Dutch masters were a joy to him and these, too, he read in the Dutch language.

He was a linguist. He was proficient in German, Dutch, Afrikaans, English, Latin and the Bantu languages. He was a dynamic leader and loyal to his people and national conscience.

He was destined to be a Member of the Representative Council. He was one of the possible candidates for the General Presidency of the African National Congress, in the event of Dr. A. B. Xuma relinquishing his position. Above all else he was an ardent Catholic. He feared God and loved his fellow men. He was a simple man like the masses.

His creative powers, his education he imparted in the Bantu Press for the benefit of his countrymen. He urged them to study and fit themselves to fight the battle against oppression. Education, he emphasized, is the gateway to high spheres: socially, politically and economically.

AN INSPIRATION

I write about this fellow man because he was great, yet very few knew about him. Most people read his name when he was no more.

I write about this fellow man because he is an inspiration. He showed that education can be acquired without the university portals.

I write about this African because the daily Press gives more space to crime and conviction, and does not tell the world that there are brilliant Africans straining mind and nerve to write a clean page against crime.

42. EDITORIAL, "Anton Lembede," *Inkundla ya Bantu,* 7 August 1947.

THE SUDDEN DEATH of Anton Lembede in Johannesburg has come as a crippling blow to the progress of the African community at a time when the demand is greatest for trained young men willing to surrender themselves completely to the service of their people.

Mr. Lembede had struggled against poverty and all the odds which stand in the way of a young African eager to forge ahead until he had passed his M.A., LL.B. degrees. After that he took over a practice which Dr. Seme had run for a number of years in Johannesburg. Going into the legal profession at a time when this was a very risky course for a young African, he rapidly won the confidence of his people as well as the Europeans with whom he dealt with in and out of Court. At the time of his death he had already set up what had very bright prospects of becoming a flourishing practice. Certainly, he had clearly shown that he would end up by being one of the greatest lawyers of our race.

Mr. Lembede's early success did not deflect him from the main purpose of his life — namely, to be a servant of his people, in the truest sense of the expression. He gave generously when financial help was asked for to advance the national cause. His own life was dedicated constantly to the service of his race. If you spoke of self-sacrifice, Anton Lembede was always the first to sacrifice himself without regard even for his own health or personal safety. In this whole make-up, there wasn't the slightest shred of selfishness.

Among a community beset with difficulties like ours these qualities speedily brought him to the forefront even in national affairs and at the time of his death, he was already a leading member of the Congress Executive Committee. His rapid success in this field naturally won him many enemies, but in his treatment of them, he was always a great man and towered a giant over them at all times. This only enhanced the respect in which he was held by all sections of our people.

In a sense, Mr. Lembede died fighting and in this respect his name will occupy a proud place among those of the fallen heroes of our race. He worked himself literally to death, to see his a free race. The example he set will guide many a coming servant of Africa. We join the many who mourn his death and in doing this are proud to salute a great son of Africa. Our race needs very many more young men and women imbued with the spirit of self-sacrifice which Mr. Lembede personified. His life and example combine to assure those of us who are living that, in the first place, he did not die in vain and that our national struggle itself is not in vain. When we show ourselves as ready to pay the price of becoming free, we shall surely shake off our ankles the shackles that bind us.

Lembede is dead, but the free Africa he always saw in his visions is a reality which will always live and those of us he has left behind can pay no better tribute to his memory than to resolve once more to carry on the fight in which he lost his life with renewed strength.

The deep sympathy of this journal and its readers goes to his bereaved relatives.

43. J. B. MARKS, "Tribute to A. M. Lembede," *Guardian,* 7 August 1947.

John B. Marks (1903–1972) was a leading figure in the ANC, the Communist Party, and the African trade union movement. After being dismissed as a teacher for his political activism, he joined the Communist Party in 1928. He studied at the Lenin School in Moscow. In the late 1940s, he served on the Central Committee of the Communist Party. He was active as well in the ANC, being elected to its national executive in 1946 and as provincial president of the Transvaal ANC in 1950. He was a key organiser of the African Mine Workers' Union and played a central role in the mine workers' strike of 1946. In 1963 he went into exile and worked in ANC offices in Tanzania until his death in 1972.

"To LIVE in hearts we leave behind is not to die."[85] In these words do I wish to pay tribute to the late Mr. Anthony [sic] Mziwakhe [sic] Lembede, M.A., LL.B., who very unexpectedly died in Johannesburg on Wednesday, July 30, 1947.

Mr. Lembede was an intellectual giant. He acquired all his degrees through private studies. He was an omnivorous reader. As a lawyer he was an uncompromising fighter. He was one of the few who proved to the world that when given the opportunity, the African could climb the academic ladder and even surpass some of the members of the so-called "superior" race.

In the domain of African politics Mr. Lembede was the embodiment of extreme African nationalism for which he, unlike many other African nationalists, never offered or dreamed of offering any apology. And this was a quality that was admired by his friends and even by those who did [not] see eye to eye with him in his extremist views.

He was founder and President of the present Congress Youth League which has sent a delegate to the world youth rally at Prague, and in the African National Congress, he allied himself very closely with the Left wing. A dynamic personality he was one of the few Africans who would not allow political differences to develop into personal animosity. Lembede was a member of the Executive of the African National Congress.

In Congress circles throughout the four provinces it is known he was in the forefront of the fight for the boycott of all elections under the Natives' Representation Act of 1936.

Those of us who shared his views give him the assurance that what he has left incomplete we shall complete.

To the critics I say let us write the late Lembede's virtues in brass and his vices, if any, on water. Farewell Lembede; Farewell.

44. GOVAN MBEKI, "A Grievous National Loss," *Inkundla ya Bantu*, 27 August 1947.

Born in Nqamakwe, Transkei, Govan Mbeki (1910–   ) earned a B.A. at Fort Hare in 1937 and a B.Econ. at the University of South Africa in 1940. He taught for several years at Adams College, where his future wife, Epainette, was a student, before he opened a cooperative store in Idutywa. From 1938 to 1944, he was editor of Territorial Magazine, *the forerunner of* Inkundla ya Bantu. *He was also active in Transkei politics, serving a four-year term in the Bunga and as secretary of the Transkei Organised Bodies. A socialist since his student days at Fort Hare, he did not join the South African Communist Party until the late 1950s. In the 1950s he continued his journalistic career, writing for political newspapers. He also was active in the ANC leadership in the Eastern Cape. He became a key figure in the ANC's armed wing,* Umkonto we Sizwe, *but was arrested in the Rivonia raid in 1963 and sentenced to a life term. Released from prison in 1988, he has remained an active figure in South African politics and is currently serving as Deputy President of the Senate. Among his publications are* South Africa: The Peasants' Revolt *(1964),* Learning from Robben Island: The Prison Writings of Govan Mbeki *(1991), and* The Struggle for Liberation in South Africa: A Short History *(1992).*

THE SHOCKING news of the most untimely death of A. M. Lembede has overshadowed the most pressing problems affecting Africans.

His death is a grievous national loss in which the African public has lost one of its most zealous and determined sons who dedicated his short span of life to the cause of his people.

In his selfless struggle for the national cause he has built himself a monument in the hearts of his people. His name will live eternally in the history of his people. His memory will ever be a source of strength to all Youth to devote themselves as he has exemplified to the most sacred and most sublime of all causes — the liberation of their people. We extend deep sympathy to his relatives and friends.

45. A. P. MDA, "The Late A. M. Lembede, M.A., (Phil) LL.B.," *Bantu World*, 27 September 1947.

Ashby Peter Mda (1916-1993) was born in the Herschel district on the Lesotho border. Educated in Catholic schools at Aliwal North and Mariazell, he moved to the Witwatersrand in 1937, where he took up a teaching position at St. John Berchman, a Catholic primary school, in Orlando Township. In the late 1930s, he became active in the African National Congress and was one of the leading figures in the founding of the ANC Youth League in 1944. When Lembede died, Mda was selected as his successor as president of the Youth League. In 1947 he decided to study for the law. He took up a teaching position at Pius XII College in Lesotho and then moved back to Herschel district. In poor health, he stepped down as Youth League president in 1949, but remained active behind the scenes as an advocate of African nationalism. In 1962, he left South Africa for Lesotho, where he practiced law until his death in 1993.

AN OLD GREEK saying runs: "They die young whom the Gods love."[86] Young Anton Muziwakhe Lembede, one of the most brilliant students that this country has produced, died "before his prime." He died at the tender age of 33, on the threshold of a scholastic, legal and political career that might have been unparalleled in Black Africa. The story of his life reads like an epitome from some lost romance; and in this article I am hoping to give the reading public a birds-eye-view of some of the major phases in his life.

Anthony [sic] M. Lembede was born in January 1914, at a farm near Nkambathweni [Camperton] in the district of Georgedale, Natal. His father, Martin Mbazwana Lembede of the AmaChunu Tribe, married Martha Nora Luthuli, when the latter was teaching at Mgwarumbe. She had previously taught respectively at Vredeville, Darlington and Umlazi Bridge after passing her Std. [Standard] V, at the Georgedale school. The family then settled at Nkambathweni, where they worked as farm labourers. It is here that Anton Muziwakhe was born. His mother who, as already stated, had had a smattering of education, began to teach her son at home. Under her tuition he managed to pass Std. II after many ups-and-downs. A present of a goat from her husband rewarded her labours.

There were many other families working on this and other neighbouring farms. Children were also employed as farm hands, and they put on sack cloth because of lack of proper clothing. The Lembedes did not like the idea of their children, working from morn till eve, clothed in hessian sacks. So they went to settle at Isabelo, where their children could attend school.

MUZIWAKHE GOES TO SCHOOL

Muziwakhe went to school for the first time at Isabelo. He was then already in Std. III and his teacher, Miss Sibeko[87] (now Rev. Sister Bernadette Sibeko of Mariannhill)[88] did much to make her new recruit at home in school. After passing his Std. III he worked for some time "in the kitchen" at Marievale, in order to get money to buy books and other school requirements. Then he proceeded to the Imbumbulu School where he did his Std. IV under Mr. Mhlongo. Thereafter he did both Standard V and VI at the Imbumbulu Intermediate School.

His tireless energy and zeal for work had already attracted widespread attention. When he passed his Std. VI in the first class, Mr. Hamilton Makhanya[89] (now Supervisor of Schools) used his influence to get Muziwakhe a bursary tenable at Adam's College,[90] Amanzimtoti, where after a brilliant career, Lembede completed his third year teachers' course in 1935. The occasion was marked by the slaughter of an ox at his home, and Reverend Ntansi of the American Board Mission, who was invited to officiate, prophesied thus: "This child will be like manna to his people. Great things are expected of him."

Those who were with him at Adams speak highly of his devotion to duty, and of his amazing brilliance. Mr. Makhanya, who has been like a father and a guardian to Lembede says that he suspected from Muziwakhe's youthful days, that great things were likely to come of his life. These opinions are more than confirmed by Jordan K. Ngubane, the editor of the "Inkundla" and a life long friend of the late Anton Lembede.

ANTON FACES THE WORLD

Although his mother was opposed to Lembede going too far afield, the young school master elected him to teach at Utrecht. Later he transferred to Newcastle.

Here he made a lasting friendship with Father W. Ochs,[91] O.M.I., who was then of the St. Lewis Bertrand's Catholic Mission, Newcastle. It was here that he began to take his studies very seriously. He already had an aim to qualify as a Lawyer. Here also he had his first illness of his life. He was taken to McCords [sic] Hospital[92] in Durban where after receiving his last sacraments of the Catholic Church, he underwent an operation of appendix. Fortunately he recovered speedily. He then transferred to Parys, O.F.S., where he became principal of the Bantu United School. A friend of his, Mr. Victor Khomari, now at the Bantu United School, Batho Location, Bloemfontein, has pleasant memories of their stay together at Parys. At this time Mr. Lembede was already busy at his bachelors degree which, however, he completed when he was at the Heilbron Secondary School, Orange Free State. Here also he made many friends including Mr. B. M. Khaketla,[93] B.A., the Basotho [sic] Dramatist-Novelist who now teaches at the Basutoland High School in Maseru.

In 1941, whilst still teaching at Heilbron, he had a major abdominal operation; so that although he made a phenomenal recovery, his digestive system remained weak. That perhaps explains his sudden death after a very brief illness. He had passed his LL.B. (bachelor of laws) when in 1943 he came to Johannesburg to be articled to Dr. P. ka I. Seme, B.A., LL.B. an attorney of long-standing in Johannesburg.

HIS LAST WORDS

In 1945 he completed his articles and in that same year, he presented his thesis for his Masters Degree in Philosophy. After a final oral examination before three judges on June 4, 1946, he emerged as a fully-fledged lawyer. Thus began a legal career that held great promise for the suffering African people.

On the morning of 29 July, 1947, he fell ill at his office in town and was taken to the Coronation Hospital where he died at about 5:30 a.m. on Wednesday, July 30, 1947.

Here are his last words recorded by a nurse who attended him during his last hours. "My brother Nicholas[94] should take care of my mother, for I am taking the same path which my forefathers took. My brother Victor should do all the good so that he can lead the African Nation. God bless you all."

HIS BRILLIANT SCHOLASTIC CAREER

When paying tribute to Mr. A. M. Lembede, in the columns of a newspaper in September, 1945, Mr. J. G. Malie[95] called him "a wonder boy" whilst Mr. J. K. Ngubane, in the columns of another paper called him "the best educated African." Nor were these lavish tributes; Lembede has as yet to find a scholastic peer. Certainly a man who at the age of 31, manages not only to pass the LL.B. within two years of his passing B.A. but also to do M.A. (philosophy) within two years of passing LL.B. is undoubtedly and unquestionably an unrivalled genius. In 1937 he passed Matric with distinction in Latin, exactly two years after passing his T4.

He then did his B.A. in three years' time passing it in 1940 with Roman Law and Logic and Metaphysics as his majors. In 1942 he obtained a pass in his degree of Bachelor of Law; and in 1944, he wrote five papers for his Master of Arts Degree.

In June 1945, he submitted his thesis for his Master's Degree on: "The Conception of God as expounded by, and as it emerges from the writings of philosophers from Descartes to the present day."

Professor Forsyth,[96] one of his examiners, sent him a congratulatory letter and gave him a book of philosophy for outstanding achievement.

I read through his thesis before he submitted it. I must confess I was taken aback by the breadth of learning and the profundity of so young a man as Anton. He found no difficulty in compassing the immeasurable regions of thought traversed by such intellectual giants as St. Augustine, St. Thomas Aquinas, Spinoza, Nietzsche, Hegel, Joad,[97] Kant and others. Not only did he summarise their main ideas on the theme, but he drew his own conclusions in a work crammed with closely-reasoned hypotheses and marked with great erudition.

Mr. Lembede was also a student of languages. He knew Latin, German and Nederlands, was busy at French.

ANTON LEMBEDE THE CATHOLIC

Lembede was deeply religious. During the funeral service which was held in the Church of Christ the King, Orlando, Rev. Father G. Martin,[98] O.M.I. paid a glowing tribute to his sterling qualities as a Christian. "He now lies in his eternal rest as a true soldier of Christ," he said.

He was baptised by Father Cyprian on September 10, 1927 at the Catholic Church, Georgedale, on the same day as his father and his brother Nicholas.

THE NATIONALIST

Anton Lembede had a deep and almost fanatical love for Africa. He would say, "I am one with Africa. Look at my face; it is black like the soil of Africa."

On another occasion, he would say, "I live for the freedom of my people, and I shall die for Africa's freedom." His ideas on the National Struggle, were crystallized in his doctrine of "Africanism," which embodied the vision of a new Africa emerging great and victorious, out of the turmoil and conflict of the National Liberation Struggle. His outlook was Pan-African, and he believed that Africa had a divine destiny, and that in due time Africa would take her rightful place among the peoples of the earth.

The African National Congress Youth League manifesto, which he drew up jointly with Jordan K. Ngubane and which the National Leader, Dr. A. B. Xuma approved, set down some of these ideas, especially in the creed of "Nationalists" at the end of the manifesto. The motto is: "Africa's Cause Must Triumph."

Lembede made his first important declaration of African Nationalism at a meeting called at the Mooki Memorial School in February, 1944. He made subsequent declarations at the first conference of the Youth League in April 1944 at the Bantu Men's Social Centre, where after an erudite exposition he showed Africa's middle position in relation to the materialistic West and the Spiritualistic Orient.

Another important speech was that delivered at the October conference of the Youth League in 1945, in which he expounded the thesis of "Africanism." But of all these speeches, the most significant was his last address, given at a reception in Orlando, on July 27, 1947. In the course of his address he made a powerful attack upon the colour ideology of this country, and proved to the hilt that the African was equal in all respects to any other nation, race or people on the face of the earth. In effect he attacked the inferiority complex from which so many Africans suffer.

LEMBEDE THE CONGRESS MAN

Lembede entered Congress politics in 1943. In 1944, he was elected to the presidency of the Congress Youth League in succession to Dr. W. Nkomo, then a medical student at the University of the Witwatersrand. Both as Congress Youth Leaguer and as a member of the Orlando branch of the Congress, and as Assistant-Secretary in the Transvaal Provincial Executive of the Congress, he did a lot to fight for the rights of the people, while attempting to strengthen Congress. At the 1946 Annual Congress Conference at Bloemfontein, he was elected to the National Executive Committee of which he died a member.

Lembede was an enemy of all forms of oppression; he did not spare himself in his attempts to strengthen the national movement. In his own writings in the press he taught the people the value of unity. His voice at the people's meetings will be missed. Thus, added poignancy attaches to the words quoted by Arthur Barlow when he commented on an article in which Walter M. B. Nhlapo paid tribute to the late Lembede: "In the garden of life, a bird sang from the highest branch, and then soared away."[99]

LEMBEDE THE LAWYER

At the time of his death, Lembede had practised for at least eleven months. He had already gained prominence along the Reef as a rising lawyer of no mean capability, and his clientele had grown by leaps and bounds. One thing about him was that he took great care in the preparation of his cases. What with his great volume of knowledge of legal theory he might with practice and experience, have risen to the highest position in the legal profession. He won many interesting cases as a result of which he became popular among large sections of the people. Mr. Templeton T. Ntwasa, a practising attorney in Johannesburg, relates an interesting story of how Lembede won the admiration of a Roodepoort Magistrate because of a case which he defended there in fluent Afrikaans. Just before his death, Lembede scored another victory at a Vereeniging Court. Up-to-date, a great number of Springs residents are loud in their praise of Lembede's legal prowess. Yet he was only beginning; he was on the threshold of his career.

LEMBEDE THE MAN

"Lembs," as he was fondly called by his wide circle of friends, was a kind and large-hearted man. Among his friends are numbered some of the humblest and simplest folks. Although he discouraged "beggary," he nevertheless was so generous, that he was known to give alms to the poor, particularly during the winter months. He himself boasted of his humble moments. He would say in some of his happiest moments: "I am proud of my peasant origin. I am one with Mother Africa's dark soil. I am Africa's own child."

His tastes also were singularly simple. The foibles, fads and fashions of sophisticated urban society did not appeal to him. "My heart yearns for the glory of an Africa that is gone. But I shall labour for the birth of a new Africa, free and great among the nations of the world," he would say.

He was, however, sometimes unapproachable on account of a mood of deep gloom, which settled on him at certain times. Some people mistakenly attributed this to arrogance. Personally I do not know what caused the dark cloud to pass momentarily over his life. Whether it was an inner pain gnawing at his very vitals, or whether it was a tragic consciousness of the fate of his downtrodden people, that caused this, the world will never know. But of one thing I am certain, and that is that it was a new thing in him. Possibly his first operation followed in 1940 by the death of his father affected him; and possibly also, his gloom was deepened by the experience of his second and more critical abdominal operation.

These things must be taken into consideration in sizing up his personality. However, these moods were only temporary phases. He was in his nature a happy soul. His dynamic and meteoric personality influenced anyone who knew him well. I have never seen a man with a more hearty laugh; he saw jokes in the most unexpected places. His friends will remember him for his characteristic laugh, which was loud and robust. His humour was the direct, simple and sincere type that went straight to the mark.

CONCLUSION

The life and death of the late Lembede has some lessons for the growing generation. First we must learn from Lembs, that success is the fruit of labour. Therefore we should apply ourselves to nobler and greater tasks in the cause of Africa's freedom.

Secondly, we must learn the value of religion, especially the christian religion in the life of individuals, peoples and nations. Our national liberation struggle must be strengthened by an unflinching faith in the Almighty God.

That we continue the struggle for national freedom with vigour, inasmuch as "Lembs" himself was a great fighter for the people's freedom.

Fourthly, as the last words of "Lembs" show, it was his desire that his brother Victor[100] who is in J.C. Form I at Mariannhill, should ultimately lead the African nation in one field or another. It is therefore the duty of the nation, especially the Youth of South Africa to see to the education of this boy who is reputed to be as brilliant as his late brother.

Lastly, the Youth of South Africa are in duty bound to perpetuate the name of Lembede in one way or another.

> "Lives of great men all remind us,
> We can make our lives sublime;
> And departing, leave behind us,
> Foot-prints on the sands of time."
> (Longfellow)[101]

46. J. A. MOKOENA, "Gone Ere his Prime Some Account of the Remarkable Career of the Late Anton Lembede," *South African Outlook,* 1 September 1947.

Joseph A. Mokoena was an active member of the Youth League in the 1940s. Born in Johannesburg, he did his schooling at St. Peter's Secondary School and Ft. Hare, where he completed his B.S. in 1941 majoring in physics and mathematics. He followed this with an M.S. at the University of South Africa and a Ph.D. from the University of the Witwatersrand. He taught at Ft. Hare from 1945 to 1957. After he left South Africa, he took up posts in Ghana, Nigeria, England, Rhodesia, and Zambia. He died in 1969.

ON THE 30th July, 1947, there passed away at the Coronation Hospital, Johannesburg, a young man by name Anton Muziwakhe Lembede. The cause of death was cardiac failure. Our African newspapers contained little or no details about the career of this man whose life came to an abrupt end at the age of thirty-three.

Anton was born in January, 1914 at the farm Nkambathini, or Georgedale, in Natal. His mother (who had only passed Standard V) taught him the elements of the three R's until he reached the Standard II stage. Thereupon he took Standard II with a certain Miss Sibeko who is now a Roman Catholic nun at Mariannhill. He passed Standard IV, V and VI in a country school at Mbumbulu, where his family is at present domiciled. He was able, by virtue of a first class pass in Standard VI, to obtain a scholarship to Adams College. There he entered for the T4 Teachers Course, and decided to pursue by private study the Junior Certificate course concurrently with his teachers' course. In his J.C. curriculum he included Afrikaans, Latin and Sesotho — languages all new to him. By dint of diligent application to his studies he passed both the T4 and the J.C. in 1935.

Economic stringency rendered it necessary that he aspire to no further 'schooling' and that he go out to start earning a living as a teacher. While teaching he continued with his private studies and secured the Matriculation certificate in 1937, with distinction in Latin.

The pursuit of a degree course at Fort Hare was not possible for him on account of the dependence of his family upon him. It was at this stage that Anton felt with definiteness the urge to study law. He embarked on a Bachelor of Arts degree course by private study, including as major subjects Philosophy and Roman Law. This degree was obtained at the end of 1940 — the lapse of time from the Matriculation being the three years normally taken by our students resident in Fort Hare. Two years later Lembede obtained his Bachelor of Laws degree.

By this time he had decided to abandon the teaching profession completely and to devote himself to law. He served his articles under Dr. I. P. ka Seme in Johannesburg; and was eventually admitted to the bar in 1946. Meanwhile he had submitted a thesis for the degree of Masters of Arts of the University of South Africa in 1945. The title of it was "The conception of God as expounded by Great Philosophers from Descartes to the present day." The thesis was accepted.

That, in brief, is a description of his academic career. His life's work — viz. the legal practice — was restricted to barely a year or so.

I intend to discuss the significance of this man under one or two heads: —

1. As a scholar: We may well admire the dogged determination of a man who from the very lowest ranks rises to heights of academic distinction, without the assistance of lecturers to act as his guides.

I make bold to say — although it may perhaps be conjecture on my part — that several of our present generation of students would find themselves hard put to it to demonstrate that same capacity for mental discipline. Lembede was too preoccupied with the important things in life to find time for trivialities. I do not know how many of our students make serious efforts to rise above the trivial. I trust they realise the importance of their being able to attend a university college. The future well being of the African peoples in this country is inevitably bound up — however imperceptibly — with the general tone prevailing at Fort Hare and other colleges. While yet we must not set ourselves aloof from the mass of our people, on the other hand we cannot allow ourselves to be dragged into the mire by those not as fortunate as ourselves, and let them prescribe standards of behaviour to us.

There is, however, another aspect that I would like to touch upon. It is often said by many that external students of the university can, by mere "swotting up" of facts, obtain such degrees as they wish to acquire, while remaining themselves quite shallow. I suggest that to achieve distinguished passes in branches of learning such as law and philosophy, a man requires something more than the mere ability to "cram" up notes.

It may also be said that the external student has missed the privilege of moving in the academic atmosphere of the university college. My personal contacts with Lembede marked him out as a man of remarkable breadth of vision and depth of knowledge.

It may be argued by others, then, that he was a mere freak of Nature. We are not unacquainted with the number of "myths" that supposedly surround the scene in which the African gropes in search of learning. There are a hundred-and-one things that are assumed, by those who cannot think deeply, to be beyond the capacity of the "Native mind." When a "Native" does rise to distinction, we must needs pause to consider whether he is not a mere irregularity of Nature, proving the rule that, as a general case, his race is incapable of rising to certain heights.

When we examine the bases on which humanity sets its actions in life, we observe how many are the hypotheses we employ in our reasoning and, how many of these are coloured more by sentiment than by the intention to clarify situations and to present the truth as it stands.

To us in this quarter of the globe, there is at once apparent the striking abuse of racial differences. In this matter we probably all come in for some share of blame. But there does exist the hypothesis that because a man belongs to a particular racial group, it is by that mere fact predetermined what his capacity in all directions will be. And when the hypothesis has been made, it becomes embarrassing to explain away aberrations that subsequently occur.

Only consistent devotion to duty and selfless application to tasks set can establish in the eyes of other groups the fact that we can do certain things. The African will live to demonstrate that he is capable of achievement on a high plane, and for the purpose of gaining this end he must look to himself. Some of us treat with contempt any suggestion that we cannot achieve greatness, and the determination is in us to put in efforts ever higher to justify our claim. Lembede demonstrated beyond doubt a mental capacity almost amounting to genius.

2. The second aspect of Lembede views him as a lawyer: He had

the advantage, as a practising lawyer, of being able to express himself fluently in both official languages of the country. To those of us who are acquainted with the manner in which state departments conduct their routine affairs, especially in connection with the African, it is at once evident what a powerful tool we had in Lembede. We take pride in the fact that Lembede, already, within so brief a period, was winning respect among the members of the Johannesburg bar.

The young men entering the field of law have embarked on a new venture. The legal profession has only now attracted a fair number; and with the obvious dangers and difficulties that lie before pioneers in any field, we require men of integrity and strength of purpose to enter the sphere and establish in their colleagues a firm faith, confidence and respect.

Lembede was such a man. He showed promise of establishing a flourishing practice; and he had already convinced his people that they could depend on him.

3. Thirdly, with reference to the African political scene, I would say that no account of Lembede's life would be complete, if it does not include a paragraph or two on his outlook on inter-racial affairs in South Africa.

For what I have said, it would appear, that here we had a man who might have been a powerful instrument to assist in solving the problem of racial differences and animosity.

He was a staunch member of the African National Congress and president of the African National Congress Youth League. In both these bodies he was a vital force with which to reckon. He represents, to my mind, that section of our youth who feel that the older generation at the helm should adopt bolder methods of tackling our problems.

We are, no doubt, aware of the reaction that usually opposes a man with new ideas and vigorous enthusiasm; and I think that in time Lembede would have found himself waging a war for ascendancy in the matter of piloting our African affairs through the deep and difficult waters.

He was a man of an impetuous nature, always determined to see through any scheme to which he set his attention. I formed the impression that he might need some curbing in his impatience if we were really going to get things done. He had strong Nationalistic views in the expression of which he went the whole way.

We may condemn the plea of "African first"; but I am not too sure that in some of us it is not engendered by motives as noble as those that gave rise to "Rule Britannia." National consciousness seems to be a factor that will for ever inspire the peoples of the world. It may be posed that the panacea for the world's ills lies in world government, such as is envisaged in the United Nations Organisation, rather than in national isolationism.

Yet there is still evident the tendency, if not the determination on the part of individual nations to have their voice heard as the voice of a specific unit.

The African is not to be blamed, therefore, if he passes through the same stages of development that have characterized the upward surge of other nations in the past.

Lembede was one of our men who chose the more difficult course of plunging into the heart of the struggle, so as to tackle problems at close quarters. Such a man must necessarily lay himself open to criticism. I am convinced that in addition to, or rather over and above, those of us who enjoy the comparative ease of academic seclusion, such men of mettle are required to engage the enemy in active combat.

It is not necessary for me to carve a legendary figure of this man. His actions speak for themselves. My firm belief is that he would, by our present standards, have made a great leader.

In his death Africa has lost a great son. We trust that others will follow the trail that he has blazed.

47. JORDAN K. NGUBANE, "A Nation's Tribute to a Promising Son," *Inkundla ya Bantu,* 17 September 1947.

Educated at Adams College and a classmate of Lembede's, Jordan Ngubane (1917–1985) was the editor of Inkundla ya Bantu. *He went into exile in Swaziland in 1961 just before he was to be served with a banning order. Later he lectured at several universities in the United States before returning to South Africa in 1980 to become an adviser to KwaZulu Chief Minister*

Mangosuthu Buthelezi. Among his publications are An African Explains Apartheid *(1963)*, Ushaba *(1974), and* Conflict of Minds *(1979)*.

THERE ARE blows from which it is possible to recover quickly; there are others which leave a gaping wound in one's soul for a lifetime. This is as true of individuals as it is of nations and in this regard the death of Anton Lembede in Johannesburg a short while ago was a blow to our race which has left a mark for all to see on the outlook of the nation.

He died still a young man — just turned thirty-two [sic]. But he had shown great promise within the three and a half years he had spent in Johannesburg. When he died, every section of our community came to pay its respects. The most moving scene of all to me, was the meeting held at the Community Hall, Orlando where representatives from every department of African life spoke in testimony of the value of the late Anton to the community. There was Mr. Sofasonke Mpanza,[102] that remarkable figure who embodies in himself the ideals for which Anton lived and fought. Mr. Templeton Ntwasa, a legal colleague, expressed the feelings of the dozens of young men in the legal profession who have lost a trusted friend and colleague. Mr. Joseph Malepe[103] spoke for the Youth of our race for he had taken part with the deceased in the formation of the Congress Youth League. Cr. Paul Mosaka[104] gave a scholarly address befitting the occasion when we had come to bury one of our greatest scholars.

So also did Dr. Wallet B. Vilakazi.

WORD OF CHEER

Rev. O. S. D. Mooki has his own way of speaking to the heart of those he addresses. Lembede's personal friend, Mr. A. P. Mda and the present author said a few words. From Dr. W. F. Nkomo, another promising young man who had started the League with Lembede, came a word of cheer that we can keep the memory of Lembede alive by keeping his ideals alive. I shall not forget Mr. E. Monoangaha[105] [sic], a leading figure in the shanty-town movement who, in the liquid Sesotho of the South, there and then launched the Anton Lembede Law Scholarship for Basutoland; Dr. Dadoo[106] too spoke.

MOVING EPISODE

But to me, the most moving episode came when Dr. Xuma rose to speak. To him, the death of Anton Lembede was a national calamity in the sense that he had seen in the young man an instance where the African had proved his capacity to overcome obstacles within South Africa and in spite of these to rise to the top. He saw Lembede's death from the perspective of history and as a general in command of a poorly equipped and badly disciplined army. At the head of the African national liberatory movement if an outstanding and capable lie[u]tenant dies, that is a loss to the supreme command of the national liberation army. And as he thought to himself, Dr. Xuma felt the nation cannot afford these losses. When he broke completely under emotional stress, he was expressing the feelings of his people as an oppressed group. Dr. P ka I. Seme, without whom we might not have known of Lembede as a national figure, spoke last.

Over fifty private cars, 25 lorries and six municipal double-decker buses carried hundreds of Africans who, by their presence, paid tribute to one of the most promising sons of our race.[107]

48. DR. W. F. NKOMO, "Tribute to a Victorious Life," *African Advocate*, August/September 1947.

Born in Makapanstad near Pretoria, the son of a Wesleyan Methodist minister and teacher, William Frederick Nkomo (1915–1972) did his schooling at St. Cyprian's, St. Peter's, and Ft. Hare, earning a B.Sc. in Biology, Zoology, and Botany in 1937. He moved on to a teaching post at Kilnerton Secondary School in Pretoria (1938–41). Nkomo's leftist leanings were evident in the 1930s when he applied for a passport to attend a World Youth Peace Congress in New York in 1939, but the government turned him down on the grounds that his traveling companions, Dr. Max Joffe and Saura Leslie, were known Communists and the Congress was a Communist front. He studied medicine at the University of Witwatersrand. completing his degree in 1946, and set up a practice in Lady Selborne. He was one of the founders of the ANC Youth League, but later broke with the ANC. He participated in the Moral Rearmament Movement and traveled abroad to their conferences.

In 1972 he was elected president of the South African Institute of Race Relations, the first African to serve as president.

KINDLY ALLOW me a space in your esteemed paper, *The African Advocate,* to add a word to the tribute already given in respect of the late Mr. Anton Muziwakhe Lembede, M.A., LL.B.

I knew him rather well in the last years of his life, a period during which we collaborated in the interests of African Youth. He was one of the young men with whom we founded the African Youth League of which I had the honour of being its first President. The work of this movement soon grew to such an extent that someone who could spare the time was required to lead the Congress Youth League. There could have been no better choice than that of Anthony [sic] Lembede. A protagonist of a new philosophy of Africanism, in contradistinction to that of Marcus Garvey,[108] Lembede was imbued with the spirit of liberating his people from the chains of oppression. He was a sincere and honest student, one who always sought to learn and know the truth, one who stood on his ground solidly in support of what he honestly considered to be right.

As a scholar, he exhibited rare qualities. A self-made man, he managed to climb the rungs of the ladder of progress until he got to the peak of academic achievement. No wonder he won the admiration of both black and white, as well as that of persons who disagreed with his political and other views.

He was exemplary to the Youth of Africa in many respects. We shall not be able to fill the gap created by his passing. Let us, however, not let his teachings fade — his life was certainly worth emulating.

49. ORGANISING SECRETARY, Congress Youth League, Statement, *African Advocate,* August/September 1947.

THE DEATH of Anton Muziwakhe Lembede, scholar, philosopher, lawyer, leader and the President of the African National Congress Youth League removes from the earth one of the greatest Sons of Africa. It deprives the African Nation of its foremost champion in the struggle for emancipation.

The late Anton Lembede had a great vision of a new Africa, emerging as a world power out of the turmoil and conflict of struggle. He had an unshakable belief in the divine destiny of Black Africa, and in the ability of the African peoples to rise to a position of greatness among the peoples of the earth. This vision and this deep faith was enshrined in his concept of African Nationalism, which he sometimes referred to as Africanism.

The African National Congress Youth League herewith pledges unalterable devotion and loyalty to this great heritage of ideals which the late leader bequeathed to African Youth. His lamented death does not leave us bereft of hope, however, for though he lies mingled in the dust, his spirit remains, and it will haunt Black Africa for centuries and centuries to come.

The Congress Youth League believes that Anton Lembede's death has an imperishable message to African Youth: "It is a trumpet call to all Youth to gird their loins and carry on the struggle for the freedom of Africa." The best tribute we can pay to the late Lembede is to emulate his great example. The best homage we can pay to his undying memory is to tread the path he trod for many a bitter year.

"The League invokes Almighty God to give his soul eternal rest and let perpetual light shine, and calls upon African Youth throughout South Africa to join in spirit with the Congress Youth League in paying their last tribute to Anton Lembede."

50. A. P. MDA, "Tribute to the late A. M. Lembede," *Imvo Zabantsundu,* 7 August 1948.

ON JULY 26 [30] a year ago, death removed from Africa one of her most illustrious sons. The death of A. M. Lembede, M.A., LL.B. meant a severe loss in the cause of the freedom of the Black People.

He has however left behind him a vivid example of self-application and his self-sacrifice for his people will be long cherished and long remembered. It will remain a constant source of inspiration to the rising hosts of young men and women who want to devote their talents and energies to the service of Africa.

The late Lembede was the first to give clear emphasis to the creed of African Nationalism and he thus crystallized and gave impetus to the forces of African National freedom.

By his brilliant academic attainments he added one more proof of the black man's ability to scale the lofty heights of achievement.

He was a staunch Congress man and he contributed greatly towards rebuilding the Congress firstly as a member of the Transvaal Provincial Committee, and secondly as a member of the National Executive.

YOUTH MUST FOLLOW SUIT

In 1943 the A.N.C. Annual conference passed a resolution to the effect that Youth Leagues should be established as integral wings of the National Congress.

The late A. M. Lembede was one of the young men who became responsible for launching the Congress Youth League in 1944. He was its first president.

The Congress Youth League has therefore every reason to be proud of his achievements; it has every reason to look up to him for inspiration.

We African Nationalists of the Congress Youth League salute the dead hero and in doing so we appeal to the African Youth throughout South Africa to follow suit.

Towards the close of the year we hope to have the first Lembede Memorial Service at which we shall formally launch a Lembede Tombstone Fund to be followed sometime next year by a Lembede Scholarship Fund Campaign.

51. "ANNIVERSARY TRIBUTE," Issued by the National Working Committee, Congress Youth League, *Inkundla ya Bantu,* 13 August 1949.

ANTON MUZIWAKHE LEMBEDE died on 30th July. 1949 is the second anniversary of his death.

The National Working Committee of the Congress Youth League issued the following statement to commemorate his death: —

"Two years ago to-day, death removed from this earth one of the greatest sons of Africa, the late Anton Muziwakhe Lembede. Not only did he leave behind him a record of an unsurpassed scholastic career which will always be an inspiration to the rising generations of Africa Youth, but he also left us a legacy of uncompromising struggle in the cause of a great, free and truly democratic Africa. His political outlook was enshrined in the creed of "Africanism" or African Nationalism which visualised a free Africa marching with the other free peoples of the earth towards progress and happiness for all mankind.

Two years after his death, we witness the forces of African Nationalism gathering momentum. The cry is beginning to be taken up everywhere: "Africa's cause must triumph!"

"This second anniversary is a trumpet-call to African Youth, in the Universities, Colleges and schools, on the mines and in the factories, and farms, in the teaching field, in the ministry and in fact everywhere, to rally round the banner of African nationalism and 'Unite for Freedom.'"

Notes

1. Booker T. Washington's educational philosophy of self-help and vocational and technical training inspired a generation of black and white educators responsible for African education in South Africa. For details, see R. Hunt Davis, "The Black American Educational Component in African Responses to Colonialism in South Africa," *Journal of Southern African Affairs* 3 (1) 1968: 69-84 and "John L. Dube: A South African Exponent of Booker T. Washington," *Journal of African Studies* 2 (1975-76): 497-528; Manning Marable, "Booker T. Washington and African Nationalism," *Phylon* 35 (1974): 398-406; and Louis Harlan, "Booker T. Washington and the White Man's Burden," *American Historical Review* 71, 2 (1966): 441-67.

2. *Lobola,* or bride price, is an African custom in which a groom gives cattle to the parents of his prospective wife. See Adam Kuper, *Wives for Cattle: Bridewealth and Marriage in Southern Africa* (London: Routledge and Kegan Paul, 1982).

3. Lembede's assertion was close to the mark. With their control over most publishing by Africans, Europeans could regulate and shape the orthography of African languages and what African writers were able to publish. See Jeffrey Peires's article on the Lovedale Press, "The Lovedale Press: Literature for the Bantu Revisited," *History in Africa,* 6 (1979): 155-175) and Brian Willan's chapter "Language and Literature: Preserving a Culture" in *Sol Plaatje: A Biography* (Berkeley: University of California Press, 1984).

4. Horace, *Satires,* Book 1, Satire 9.

5. The Representation of Natives Act of 1936 established an advisory body, the Natives Representative Council (NRC), which convened for the first time in 1937. It was composed of 22 members: the chairman (Secretary for Native Affairs), five appointed white "native" commissioners, four appointed Africans, and twelve indirectly elected African representatives (3 from the urban areas, 9 from the rural areas). The body could deliberate and offer advice on legislation affecting Africans in the European Parliament and it could propose legislation on African matters. However, the council was hamstrung from the outset. As its ineffectiveness became clear, it attracted strong opposition from within the African community, especially Youth Leaguers, who viewed the council as a talk shop and a means to con-

trol African opposition. Finally, African representatives in the council boy-
cotted it, and it was disbanded in 1951 as the National Party government began
implementing its apartheid policies. See C. M. Tatz, *Shadow and Substance in
South Africa: A Study in Land and Franchise Policies Affecting Africans,
1910-1960* (Pietermaritzburg: University of Natal Press, 1962).

6. The constitution of South Africa was ratified by the Act of Union,
passed in the British Parliament in September 1909. The act paved the way
for the creation of the Union of South Africa in May 1910.

7. The Natives Land Act of 1913 was a cornerstone of a segregated South
Africa. The law froze the unequal land division between blacks and whites by
stating that Africans could not buy European land and vice versa. It also undermined sharecropping arrangements that made it possible for some blacks
to maintain a semi-independent base on the land by restricting the number
of black heads of household who worked on European farms and stipulating
that blacks could only rent white farm land with labor service. The Act set
off a flurry of expulsions of black sharecroppers, especially in the Orange
Free State, but it took a number of years before sharecropping was a spent
institution. Solomon Plaatje's *Native Life in South Africa* (London: P. S.
King and Son, 1916) remains a classic account of the impact of the law on
Africans.

8. The Mines and Works Amendment Act of 1926 (or "Colour Bar" Act)
provided for the government to restrict certain skilled occupations on the
mines, such as operating machines, to Europeans and Coloureds.

9. Through the Native Urban Areas Act, the government sought to control African urbanization by setting up African locations separate from European residential areas, creating advisory boards to encourage a limited
form of African participation in governing, and instituting controls on trading, beer brewing, and vagrancy. See T. R. Davenport, "African Townsmen?
South African Natives (Urban Areas) Legislation Through the Years," *African Affairs* 68 (271) (1969): 95-109 and Paul Maylam, "The Rise and Decline
of Urban Apartheid in South Africa," *African Affairs* 89 (354) (1990): 57-84.

10. The Native Administration Act (1927) gave the government arbitrary
powers over Africans throughout the country, including the right to appoint
native administrators, chiefs, and headmen; to remove African "tribes" "from
any place to any other place within the Union"; to legislate by proclamation
for the African reserve areas; and to punish "any person who utters any
words or does any other act or thing whatever with intent to promote any
feeling or hostility between Natives and Europeans." This last provision was
used repeatedly to prevent African politicians from organizing by banishing
them from African areas.

11. A limited number of Coloureds and Africans who met educational, property or salary qualifications had the right to vote in elections in the Cape Province. In 1926, 14,912 Africans, 2,085 Indians, and 21,223 Coloureds had the vote in the Cape out of a total electorate of a little over 200,000. A clause in the Union constitution stipulated that the Cape franchise could not be abolished unless a two thirds majority in Parliament approved it. Prime Minister Hertzog launched his campaign to get rid of the Cape franchise for Africans in 1926, but it took him another decade before he achieved his goal.

12. The Representation of Natives Act of 1936 provided for Africans in the Cape Province to elect three members (who had to be "British subjects of European descent") to the House of Assembly. The vote was restricted to any male who owned property worth £75 or earned a salary of at least £50 per year, who was at least 21 years old, who was able to sign his name, address, and occupation, and whose name had previously appeared on the voters' role.

13. The 1936 Natives Trust and Land Act provided for the government to transfer additional or "released" land to the reserve areas so long as it was adjacent land. When the Youth League Manifesto was written in 1944, the government was just beginning to buy up land to be added to the African reserves, which comprised roughly 7 percent of the land in 1936.

14. The Native Laws Amendment Act (1937) aimed at bringing urban policy in line with the 1913 Natives Land Act. The Act provided for biennial industrial censuses in municipalities. The government intended to control the influx of blacks into urban areas and to remove "surplus" blacks from the urban areas and generally prohibit Africans from owning land in the urban areas.

15. They are referring to the lobbying for a Youth League at the 1943 Bloemfontein conference of the African National Congress. The conference passed a resolution that stated: "henceforth it shall be competent for the African youth to organise and establish Provincial Conferences of the Youth League with a view of forming a National Congress of the Youth League immediately."

16. The Manifesto is probably referring to the formation of the African Democratic Party (ADP) in 1943, which siphoned some youth support away from the ANC. The ADP's creation, however, is cited as one reason why Dr. Xuma was sympathetic to the Youth League's formation — to shore up youth support for the ANC. For more details on the ADP, see note 36.

17. Aristotle, *Politica.*

18. Bethuel Mnguni's African Youth League was started up around the same time as the ANC Youth League. Although some contended Mnguni's

group was a front for the Trotskyists, Mnguni claimed his group was independent. A presentation of the League's program is found in "African Youth League," *Inkundla ya Bantu* (28 February 1945, p. 2). The League advocated scrapping the land laws and the reserve system, poll taxes, pass laws, urban areas legislation, and the color bar and introducing free compulsory education and a universal franchise.

19. C. S. Ramohanoe was provincial president of the Transvaal African National Congress from 1944 to 1950. After J. B. Marks defeated him for the provincial presidency in 1950, he joined a breakaway faction, the Nationalist Minded Bloc, and took over as leader after Selope Thema died in 1955.

20. Alexander Pope, "An Essay on Man."

21. James Shirley, "Contention of Ajax and Ulysses."

22. Founded in 1941 by merging a number of student associations, the Transvaal African Students' Association (T.A.S.A.) involved itself in a range of activities, including sports, music, theatricals; sponsoring debates, discussions, and lectures; and sending deputations to present evidence to government commissions. T.A.S.A. briefly put out a publication, *T.A.S.A. Bulletin.* Among its members were a number of future Youth League activists.

23. Ironically, the campaign against pass laws had been launched in November 1943 by the Communist Party. In 1944, after the government moved to tighten up pass laws relaxed during the Second World War, Dr. Xuma had committed the ANC to the Anti-Pass campaign. A mass conference of 540 delegates representing 375 organizations launched the Anti-Pass Campaign, which centered on gathering one million signatures on a petition calling on the government to abolish pass laws. This goal proved difficult to achieve and the petition that was submitted to the government in June 1945 fell short of the goal. Even then, government ministers did not accept the petition. The campaign was sustained into 1946 when the ANC redirected its focus towards boycotting the Natives Representative Council. See also Lembede's comment in Document 33.

24. Born in the Pietersburg area, Richard Baloyi (c. 1897–1962) was a successful Alexandra real estate agent who played an active role in civic and political affairs. He served as treasurer-general of the ANC from 1938 to 1949 and was a member of the Natives Representative Council from 1937 to 1942. In the early 1950s he was associated with Selope Thema's Nationalist Minded Bloc, composed largely of former ANC leaders who were unhappy with the ANC's growing ties with Coloured and Indian political organizations.

25. Born in Pietersburg area, David W. Bopape (1915–   ) was educated at Botshabelo Training College, Middelburg. He was active in the Transvaal African Teachers' Association (TATA) and was secretary of the TATA

campaign for higher salaries and better conditions of service that was high-lighted by a mass protest march in downtown Johannesburg in 1944. For his participation in the teachers' campaign, he was dismissed as a teacher in Brakpan in 1944. Although his dismissal set off a community protest, he was not reinstated.

26. A Methodist minister based in Pimville, Rev. H. Mpitso was secretary-organizer of the African Ministers' Association. He was a leading figure in the Mendi Memorial Fund set up to commemorate the contributions of African soldiers during the First World War and the sinking of the *Mendi,* a transport ship carrying Africans, in the English channel in 1917. An active member of the ANC, he served on the African Claims committee and on its National Executive.

27. In an attempt to salvage the Natives Representative Council, Prime Minister Smuts had met with six African members of the NRC on 8 May 1947 and proposed changing the Council by making it larger and directly elected and delegating it with some responsibility for governing the re-serves. By and large, African leaders opposed his proposals. For more de-tails, see Gwendolen Carter and Thomas Karis, eds., *From Protest to Chal-lenge: A Documentary History of African Politics in South Africa, 1882-1964* (Stanford: Hoover Institution Press, 1973), Vol. II, 95-97.

28. At the 1946 ANC convention, with Xuma off on a trip to the United States, a resolution was passed instructing the ANC executive to organize a boycott of the festivities surrounding the tour of South Africa by King George V and the Royal Family. The boycott never got off the ground.

29. Edward Hickson, "Try and Try Again."

30. *Bible,* 1 Corinthians 13:11.

31. Shaka (ca. 1787-1828) was king of the Zulu Kingdom. Sekhukhune (1814-1882) was king of the Pedi nation. Moshoeshoe (ca. 1786-1870) was king of the Basotho nation. Khama (Kgama) (ca. 1837-1923) was king of the Ngwato kindgom. Sobhuza I (ca. 1830s-1839) was king of the Swazi nation. Hintsa was paramount chief of the Gcaleka Xhosa (ca. 1790-1835). Makana (Makanda) (ca. 1780s-1820) was a prophet, war leader and counsellor to the Ndlambe Xhosa. Mzilikazi (ca. 1790-1868) was king of the Ndebele nation.

32. The quote is from a May 1941 pamphlet, *Ten Articles of Faith,* by an American political correspondent and commentator, Dorothy Thompson (1893-1961). For details on her life, see Marion Sanders, *Dorothy Thompson: A Legend in Her Times* (Boston: Houghton Mifflin, 1973) and Peter Kurth, *American Cassandra: The Life of Dorothy Thompson* (Boston: Little, Brown and Co., 1990).

33. Paul Kruger made such a statement in his last will and testament just before his death in 1904.

34. Henry Wadsworth Longfellow, "A Psalm of Life."

35. The *khotla* (*kgotla*) was a Sotho/Tswana institution in which a chief called together the adult males of the "nation" to discuss issues of national importance and adjudicate disputes. *Kgotlas* were held in an open space in a village setting. Although chiefs and headmen presided over discussions, commoners theoretically had the right to voice opinions, even if they were critical of leaders. Court decisions were not based according to a legal code, but came about through negotiations which usually favored those with status and political influence. For discussions on Tswana *kgotlas* historically, see Diana Wylie, *A Little God: The Twilight of Patriarchy in a Southern African Chiefdom* (Hanover: University Press of New England, 1990) and the chapters by Leonard Ngcongco, P. T. Mgadla and A. C. Campbell, and K. Datta and A. Murray in John Holm and Patrick Molutsi, eds., *Democracy in Botswana* (Gaborone, Botswana: Macmillan Botswana Publishing Co., 1989).

36. The African Democratic Party (ADP) had been launched on 26 September 1943. Leading figures in the party were Paul Mosaka, Self Mampuru, and Dan Koza, who later resigned from the ADP. In contrast to the Youth League, the ADP had strong connections with white liberal groups such as the Friends of Africa and the South African Institute of Race Relations. One of its strongest white supporters was Hyman Basner, a lawyer and former Communist and Native Senator. The party's platform was liberal and called for peaceful negotiations with the government and the use of mass passive resistance "as a last resort." The party was a threat for a while to the ANC, and its formation was one reason why Dr. Xuma allowed the Youth League to be formed — to pull in young people who may have been attracted to the ADP. The ADP was kept alive until about 1948.

37. The Fourth International of South Africa (FIOSA) emerged in the early 1940s after a split in the Trotskyist Cape Town-based Lenin Club. FIOSA took a purist line on worker organization and opposed the Communist Party's "Native Republic" thesis, arguing that any compromise with black nationalism diluted working class unity. FIOSA's Johannesburg branch gave its support to the African Democratic Party, though not without reservations. FIOSA died out in the late 1940s.

38. A leader of the Indian National Congress and India's independence movement, Jawaharlal Nehru (1889–1964) became India's first Prime Minister, 1947–1964.

39. A lawyer and an ardent republican, Giuseppe Mazzini (1805–1872) was

a founder of Young Italy in 1831 and a leading figure in the movement for Italy's unification. Mazzini based his appeals for unification on Italian ethnicity, a contrast to Lembede's Pan African ideals. The quote comes from an address Mazzini delivered on the anniversary of the death of the Bandiera brothers and other Italian patriots, 25 July 1848. The full text of the address is found in N. Gangulee, ed., *Giuseppe Mazzini: Selected Writings* (Westport, Ct.: Greenwood Press, 1974).

40. Tuberculosis rates among Africans shot up dramatically during the Second World War. For instance, the incidence among Africans in Johannesburg increased from 1.0 per thousand in 1938 to 2.4 per thousand in 1945. See Randall Packard, *White Plague, Black Labour: Tuberculosis and the Political Economy of Health and Disease in South Africa* (Berkeley: University of California, 1989), especially chapter 8.

41. In 1947, Daniel Malan, leader of the National Party, and N. C. Havenga, leader of the Afrikaner Party, agreed on an election pact to combat Jan Smuts' United Party. In the 1948 election, the National Party won 70 seats (previously 43) and the Afrikaner Party 9 (previously none) in the House of Assembly. This represented a majority of seats and the Nationalists were able to form a government.

42. Hundreds of Africans had converged on Bloemfontein in December 1935 to form the All African Convention (AAC) to rally black opinion against the Hertzog bills, which aimed at removing Cape African voters from the common voters' role. Led by Prof. D. D. T. Jabavu, a Fort Hare lecturer, the AAC for several years eclipsed the ANC in popularity, but when it failed to live up to its promise, politicians in the Transvaal and Cape moved to rejuvenate and reorganize the ANC.

43. We have not been able to identify the author of this poem, but several Afrikaans literature specialists have independently suggested that the author was one of the Afrikaner labor poets who were active during that era.

44. This quote comes from Jean-Jacques Rousseau, *Social Contract*.

45. John Dube (1871–1946) was born at the Inanda mission station in Natal. Educated at Inanda and Amanzimtoti Training College, he went to the United States in 1887 and studied at Oberlin College. He returned to South Africa in 1892 as a teacher and became superintendent of Incwadi Christian Industrial Mission. He had a second sojourn in the U.S., studying theology from 1897 to 1899 at Union Missionary Seminary in Brooklyn. Ordained a Congregational minister, he was attracted to Booker T. Washington's ideas on industrial education and, in 1904, founded his own school, Ohlange Institute, patterned on Washington's ideals. He started a newspaper, *Ilanga lase Natal,* in 1903 and was its editor until 1915. He was also active in politics,

working in the Native National Congress and serving as the first president of the South African Native National Congress (SANNC) from 1912 until 1917 (the SANNC changed its name to the African National Congress in 1923). A conservative figure, he opposed radicalizing influences in the ANC.

46. Rev. Zacceus Richard Mahabane (1881-1970) was a Methodist minister. Elected president of the Cape ANC in 1919, he also served as president of the ANC (1924-1927, 1937-1940). He was a founding member of the AAC and its vice president in 1937.

47. Born in Krugersdorp, Obed Simon David Mooki (1919-1990) was the son of an independent church leader and founded his own church, Mooki Memorial Church, and a school in Orlando. In 1938, he was ordained a minister in the New Church, a London-based church; in 1969 he was made superintendent of the New Church Mission after it had become independent. He was a member and secretary of the Orlando Advisory Board and, in 1953, he became president of the South African Advisory Boards Congress. At various times, he was chairman of the Orlando School Board, chaplain of the Transvaal branch of the African National Congress, and president of the Transvaal Interdenominational African Ministers Association.

48. S. S. Tema (1899-1981) was born in Ga-Molepo in the Northern Transvaal. A Dutch Reformed Church minister, he pastored a church in Orlando until he took up a position as traveling secretary of the Students' Christian Association in 1941. In 1949 he moved to Pretoria where he was minister at the Atteridgeville Dutch Reformed Church. Later he served as president of the Transvaal Interdenominational African Ministers' Association. He was assistant secretary of the Johannesburg Joint Council of Europeans and Natives. He was a delegate to the Tambaran (India) international missionary conference in 1939, where he met Mahatma Gandhi. After retiring from the ministry in 1968, he was elected to the Lebowa Legislative Assembly.

49. Born in Vrededorp, Nimrod Boyce Tantsi (1895-1977) worked as an insurance agent and teacher in East London, Bloemfontein, and Johannesburg before taking up the ministry in the African Methodist Episcopal (AME) church in 1929. His father, Japie Zachariah Tantsi, and James Y. Tantsi, had been among the earliest ordained AME ministers. He served churches in Ventersdorp, Boksburg, and Atteridgeville before moving to Lady Selborne in 1939, where he established a number of schools. Later he served circuits in Orlando, Bloemfontein, Heilbron, and Springs. Active in the ANC since its early years, Tantsi was made chaplain for the Transvaal ANC and was elected Acting President of the Transvaal ANC in place of Nelson Mandela in June 1952 during the Defiance Campaign.

50. Guido Geselle was a popular Flemish poet.

51. Started in 1940, *Inkululeko* (Freedom) was an organ of the Communist Party of South Africa. It had been preceded by *The International* and the *South African Workers/Umsebenzi*. Although it regularly covered international news, it focused on news in the African community and featured columns in African languages (seSotho, Venda, Zulu). Its editors were M. S. Diphuko and Edwin Mofutsanyana. *Inkululeko* ceased publication in 1950 after the passage of the Suppression of Communism Act.

52. The three were leaders of pro-Nazi groups in South Africa. A former Minister of Justice, Oswald Pirow headed up the *Nuwe Order* (New Order). Dr. J. F. J. van Rensburg was leader of the *Ossewa Brandwag*. L. T. Weichardt was head of the Grey Shirts. He was interned during the Second World War. For more details, see Patrick Furlong, *Between Crown and Swastika: The Impact of the Radical Right on the Afrikaner Nationalist Movement in the Fascist Era* (Middletown, Conn.: Wesleyan University Press, 1991).

53. Established in 1943, the Non-European Unity Movement (NEUM) was an amalgam of various groups: the All African Convention, the Anti-CAD (Coloured Affairs Department), and the Transkei Organised Bodies. Popular among Coloured and African intellectuals mainly in the western Cape, the NEUM advocated non-collaboration with segregated institutions such as the Natives Representative Council and put forward a Ten-Point Programme (universal franchise, land redistribution, civil rights, free and compulsory education). Although Youth Leaguers were hostile to NEUM, they were influenced by its stances.

54. This undated document is to be found in the Ballinger Papers (A410, C2.3.9.1), Church of the Province Reading Room, Witwatersrand University. It states that it was written by Lembede for the Youth League.

55. Lembede is referring to a series of laws which reserved certain jobs on the mines for whites and made it impossible for African workers to advance themselves into skilled positions. Among these laws are the Mines and Works Act of 1911 and the Mines and Works Amendment Act of 1926.

56. Passed in 1924, the Industrial Conciliation Act established industrial councils made up of representatives of employers and registered trade unions, to regulate wages and conditions of service in most sectors of the economy. The legislation aimed to bureaucratize trade unions and curb their activism, but it did not prevent several militant unions from carrying on through the 1930s. The act excluded Africans from its definition of employee, and thus did not cover them. For an analysis of the act, see Robert Davies, "The Class Character of South Africa's Industrial Conciliation Legislation," *South African Labour Bulletin* 2 (6) (1976).

57. Passed in 1856 in the Cape Colony, the Masters and Servants Act's

main intent was to bind servants to masters by making it an offense for a servant to break a contract (which included desertion, insubordination, and insulting behavior). The law remained in effect until its repeal in 1974, when Alabama dock workers and miners in the United States decided not to off-load South African coal acting on an American law that prohibited the importation of goods produced by forced labor. By then, the Masters and Servants Act had been superseded by other laws controlling black employees, and it no longer served a twentieth-century purpose. See Colin Bundy, "The Abolition of the Masters and Servants Act," *South African Labour Bulletin,* 2 (May-June 1975): 37-46.

58. The Industrial and Commercial Workers' Union (ICU) had its heyday in the 1920s, when it attracted upwards of 100,000 members. ANC competition with the ICU was not the only reason for the ICU's rapid demise in the late 1920s. Other factors included Kadalie's autocratic leadership style, the personal misuse of union funds by ICU officials, the ICU's expulsion of Communists on its executive, Kadalie's associations with white liberals and his reliance on William Ballinger as an adviser, the ICU's attempt to organize workers of differing backgrounds (industrial workers and farm workers) and government persecution.

Following its collapse, the ICU broke into splinter groups. The ICU's general secretary, Clements Kadalie, moved to East London and kept an ICU branch alive there. He and a slate of ICU candidates were elected to the East London Advisory Board in the 1940s, but they did not have national pretensions. Lembede's commentary on the ICU reviving itself may have been because of a May/June 1946 strike at Buffalo Harbor, East London (which white officials attributed to Kadalie) or to reports in the press that Kadalie had submitted evidence in October 1946 to the Natives Law Commission. In any event, an ICU revival never took place.

59. The opening lines of Wordsworth's "London 1802" read: "Milton! thou shouldst be living at this hour; England hath need of thee;"

60. Selby Msimang (1886-1982) was present at the launching of the SANNC in 1912 and was one of its stalwarts over the decades. In 1920 he was elected president of the ICU, but stepped aside for Clements Kadalie to avoid an internal dispute. Educated at Edendale Training Institution and Healdtown Institution, he became an interpreter, a mine clerk, a solicitor's clerk (in Pixley Seme's office), and a journalist for *Umteteli wa Bantu.* In 1935 he became secretary of the All African Convention and was a member of the delegation that met with Hertzog to discuss the "Native" bills. He was provincial secretary of the Natal ANC (1942-1956) and on the executive of the Liberal Party (1956-1968).

60. See note 5.

61. This refers to the argument that even though the 1936 legislation did away with the Cape African franchise, there would be compensation — European representatives for Africans and a Natives Representative Council. The 1936 compromise is discussed in Saul Dubow, *Racial Segregation and the Origins of Apartheid in South Africa, 1919-1936* (New York: St. Martin's Press, 1989).

62. Founded in 1889 by the major gold mining houses, the Chamber of Mines coordinated policy on issues vital to the profitability of the gold mines such as wages and the recruitment of African labor. The chamber created a monopolistic recruiting organization, the Witwatersrand Native Labour Association, so the mining houses would not have to compete with each other and pay higher wages to black workers.

63. Born in the Reitz district of the Orange Free State, Jacob M. Nhlapo (1904-1957) was educated at Bensonvale Institution and Lovedale. After teaching at Healdtown, he moved on to Moroka High School in Thaba 'Nchu in 1930 and became its principal in 1934. He was elected vice president of the South African Native Teachers' Association. He received a B.A. from the University of South Africa in 1937 and a Ph.D. from McKinley Roosevelt University in Chicago for his dissertation on "Intelligence Tests and the Educability of the South African Bantu." He served as principal of Wilberforce Institute from 1940 to 1948 and Boitsheko High School in the western Transvaal. In 1951, he was appointed lecturer at Selly Oak Colleges in Birmingham. Following Selope Thema's death in 1953, he was appointed editor of the *Bantu World*, a position he stayed in until his death in 1957. He became a member of the ANC executive in 1944 and helped to draft *Africans' Claims*. Among his publications are *Bantu Babel* (1944), *Nguni and Sotho: A Practical Plan for the Unification of the South African Bantu Languages* (1945), and *Wilberforce Institute* (1949).

64. Dr. Alfred Bitini Xuma (1893-1962) was president of the African National Congress from 1940 to 1949. Born in Transkei, he traveled to the United States in 1913, studying at Tuskegee Institute and the University of Minnesota, where he was awarded a B.S. in 1920. He completed a M.D. degree in 1926 at Northwestern University. In 1927 he returned to South Africa, but traveled to the United States on several occasions. In 1935, he participated in the launching of the All African Convention and was selected as its Vice President. But in the late 1930s, he directed his energies to reviving the ANC and was elected its president in 1940 by a narrow margin. He centralized the ANC's operations and directed a rewriting of the ANC's constitution. He was reluctant to commit the ANC to mass action and that eventually led to his defeat for re-election as ANC president at the 1949 conference.

65. Dr. Xuma had been an undergraduate at Tuskegee Institute, Washington's school, where he would have learned about Washington's famous "Cast down your bucket where you are" speech. Washington's five-minute oration on race relations, delivered at the Cotton States and International Exposition in Atlanta in 1895, called on blacks and whites to work cooperatively with each other and for whites to open up opportunities for blacks in exchange for blacks accommodating themselves to a segregated status. A well known passage in the speech went: "In all things that are purely social we can be as separate as the fingers, yet one as the hand in all things essential to mutual progress." See Louis Harlan, *Booker T. Washington: The Making of a Black Leader, 1856-1901* (New York: Oxford University Press, 1972), pp. 204-28.

66. Born in Winston-Salem, North Carolina, Madie B. Hall met Dr. Xuma on his trip to the United States in 1937-1938. After they married in 1940, she moved to Johannesburg to join him and she stayed in South Africa until Dr. Xuma's death in 1962. She was active in ANC womens' organizations and she helped found the *Zenzele* self-help movement.

67. Born in Cofimvaba, Transkei, Templeton T. Ntwasa (1904-1961) attended Lovedale, where he gained a reputation as a fierce fast bowler in cricket, and Fort Hare, where he finished his matric and a B.A. in 1930. He worked as a clerk for the Transkeian Territories General Council. He served his articles with a Mr. Heathcote in Johannesburg and began practicing law in 1941. He left for Transkei in the late 1940s, where he set up law offices in Bizana, Flagstaff, and Mount Ayliff. An accomplished organist and pianist, he played classical music recitals at the Cathedral in Umtata. He arranged for the wedding of Winnie and Nelson Mandela at the town hall in Bizana. He also served as master of ceremonies.

68. Pixley ka I. Seme (1881-1951) was president of the ANC from 1930 to 1937. He earned a B.A. from Columbia University in 1906 and then completed his law studies at Oxford University. On his return to South Africa, he established a law firm with Alfred Mangena and was one of the founding members of the ANC. He joined with D. D. T. Jabavu in convening the All African Convention, but later turned against it.

69. In 1919 Rev. F. B. Bridgman of the American Board Mission founded the Bantu Men's Social Centre (BMSC), situated in Eloff St. Extension, to provide cultural and recreational facilities in a Christian setting for African men in and around the Johannesburg area. Peter Abraham's *Tell Freedom: Memories of Africa* (London: Faber and Faber, 1954) contains a description of the BMSC.

70. Born in 1911 at Mount Fletcher, Transkei, Victor Vincent Tamsanqa Mbobo was schooled at Lovedale and Fort Hare, where he received a B.A. in

1935. He was an ardent sportsman and rugby enthusiast. He later completed a B.Econ. in 1942 from the University of South Africa. He taught English and Latin at Healdtown and Nyaluza High School, Grahamstown before he was appointed headmaster at Hofmeyr High School, Pretoria. Active in the ANC Youth League, he briefly served on the national executive of the ANC in 1949. In 1947 he represented the Youth League at the World Federation of Democratic Youth Festival in Czechoslovakia. After qualifying as a lawyer, he set up practice at Umtata and Tsolo in Transkei before moving to East London where he died.

71. This is likely James Mdatyulwa, secretary of the Potchefstroom branch of the African National Congress and a member of the Potchefstroom Advisory Board.

72. Randall Peteni (1915–   ) was born in Keiskamahoek, Cape. He completed his high school studies at Lovedale, a B.A. (1938) at Fort Hare, and B.A. Honours and M.A. from the University of South Africa. He taught at Heilbron High School (1939–42) at the same time as Lembede as well as Orlando High School (1942–49), Hoernle School (1950–1956), Grahamstown (1958–1962), and New Brighton, Port Elizabeth (1963–68). In 1969, he joined the faculty of Fort Hare, where he taught English until his retirement in 1980. He authored *Hill of Fools: A Novel of the Ciskei* (London: Heinemann, 1976) and *Towards Tomorrow: The Story of the African Teachers' Associations of South Africa* (Algonac, Michigan: Reference Publications, 1979).

73. H. I. E. Dhlomo, *Dingane ka Senzangakhona* (Pietermaritzburg: Shuter and Shooter, 1936), Thomas Mofolo's *Chaka* (Morija: Sesuto Book Depot, 1925); John Dube, *U Jeqe, The Bodyservant of King Shaka* (Lovedale: Lovedale Press, 1951). For the plot outlines of these novels, see Albert Gerard, *Four African Literatures: Xhosa, Sotho, Zulu, Amharic* (Berkeley: University of California Press, 1971). For more details on the lives of Mofolo and Dhlomo, see Dan Kunene, *Thomas Mofolo and the Emergence of Written Sesotho Prose* (Johannesburg: Ravan Press, 1989) and Tim Couzens, *The New African: A Study of the Life and Work of H. I. E. Dhlomo* (Johannesburg: Ravan Press, 1985).

74. Benedict Wallet Vilakazi (1906–1947) was born at Groutville Mission Station, Natal. He completed his teacher's certificate at St. Francis School, Mariannhill, in 1923 and taught at Mariannhill and Ixopo Seminary. Through private study he obtained a B.A. degree from the University of South Africa in 1934. He was appointed lecturer in the Department of Bantu Studies at Witwatersrand University in 1934. He completed an M.A. in 1938 and a Ph.D. in 1946. His dissertation was titled, "The Oral and Written Literature of the Nguni." He published several novels, *Noma Nini* (1935), *UDingiswayo ka-*

Jobe (1939), and *Nje nempela* (1949), and several books of poetry, *Inkondlo ka Zulu* (1935) and *Amal'ezulu* (Zulu Horizons). He died in October 1947.

75. Bambatha's Rebellion was sparked off in 1906 by an unpopular poll tax levied on all unmarried men in Natal. The rebellion took its name from Bambatha, a minor Zulu chief in northern Natal, who led one phase of the rebellion, a guerilla campaign in the Nkandla forests. For details, see Shula Marks, *Reluctant Rebellion: the 1906–8 Disturbances in Natal* (Oxford: Clarendon Press, 1970).

76. "Ukucela intombi" means to ask a family for a woman's hand in marriage.

77. Lembede is referring to Mikro's [pseudonym for C. H. Kuhn] *Vreemdelinge* (Johannesburg: Afrikaanse Pers-Boekhandel, 1944), which centers on Coloured people, and Helene van Rhyn's *Hugenotebloed* (Pretoria: J. L. van Schaik, 1933), which dealt with the struggle of a poor white against poverty.

78. *Noma Nini* (Forever) (Mariannhill, 1935) was Vilakazi's first novel. Set during the Zulu king Mpande's reign (1840–72), the story centers around the love life of a young woman at Groutville mission.

79. Formed in 1934, *Die Afrikaanse Skrywerskring* (The Afrikaans Writers' Association) is affiliated to the international P. E. N. association. It published a quarterly, *Tydskrif vir Letterkunde,* sponsored writers' festivals and congresses and promoted Afrikaans literature. Headquartered in Pretoria, *Die Akademie vir Wetenskap en Kuns* was established in 1909 to promote Afrikaans (and Dutch). In 1941, the Academy was divided into two faculties: one for Language and Literature and the other for Science and Technology. The Language and Literature branch has been responsible for such things as monitoring Afrikaans orthography, preserving historic buildings and establishing a research wing, the Africa Institute.

80. Alexander J. Mackenzie, *Propaganda Boom* (London: J. Gifford, 1938), p. 9. Mackenzie's book dealt with propaganda techniques and strategies devised for communications (film, radio, and the press) by twentieth century governments. His examples included Great Britain, Soviet Union, Mussolini's Italy and Nazi Germany.

81. *Inkundla ya Bantu* (Bantu Forum) started as *Territorial News* in 1938, but changed its name in 1944. Published in Verulam, Natal, it was one of the few African-owned newspapers in South Africa. After Jordan Ngubane took over as editor in 1944, he tilted the newspaper's coverage towards the ANC, and Youth Leaguers especially used the newspapers as an outlet for their activities and views. *Inkundla* had a peak circulation of around 7,000 in 1946.

82. Lembede is referring to Albert Venn Dicey's *Introduction to the Study of the Constitution,* which had gone through eight editions by the

1940s. For more details on Dicey's life, see Richard Cosgrove, *The Rule of Law: Albert Venn Dicey, Victorian Jurist* (Chapel Hill: University of North Carolina Press, 1980).

83. John Dube had been the kingpin of the Natal ANC for many decades, but when ill health prevented him from continuing in active politics, his absence set off a power struggle between Dube's supporters who backed Rev. Abner M'timkulu and A. W. G. Champion, a former ICU official whose power base was in Durban's African townships. In a disputed election in 1945 that Xuma had to resolve, Champion was elected Natal ANC Congress president. However, Champion maintained his independence from Xuma's national leadership, and he did not have an amicable relationship with Youth Leaguers. In 1951, Champion was toppled by Albert Luthuli, who was elected ANC national president the following year.

84. Published fortnightly, *Inkundla ya Bantu* only became a weekly paper for a brief period in the late 1940s.

85. The original line from Thomas Campbell's "Hallowed Ground" reads "To live in hearts we leave is not to die."

86. "They die young, whom the Gods love" is a phrase that appears in several sources: Manander's *Dis Exapaton,* Plautus's *Bacchides,* and Byron's *Don Juan.*

87. Born in Ladysmith, Sister Bernadette Sibeko (1908–   ) was introduced to the Catholic church when she went for schooling at Mariannhill, where her teacher was Father Bernard Huss. She received a teachers' and university certificate there. In 1929 she joined the Catholic order of the Daughters of St. Francis of Assisi and continued with her teaching career at schools around the Mariannhill area. She has translated twenty-one books from English into Zulu, including the New Testament. In 1975 she completed a D.D. degree. She presently lives at Assisi Convent, Port Shepstone, Natal.

88. Founded by Trappist monks near Durban in 1892, Mariannhill was a center for Catholic missions and education, with dozens of schools established for Africans. Teachers such as Alfred Bryant and Bernard Huss were prominent names associated with Mariannhill education. For details on Mariannhill's history, see Francis Schimlek, *Mariannhill: A Study in Bantu Life and Missionary Effort* (Mariannhill: Mariannhill Mission Press, 1953) and *Mariannhill and Its Apostolate* (Reimlingen via Nordlingen, Germany: St. Joseph Mission Press, 1964).

89. Hamilton Makhanya (1895–1981) grew up in Durban and attended school in Victoria St. He attended Adams College and later taught there. He also taught at several schools before being promoted to school inspector. Af-

ter his retirement, he served as Secretary of the Tribal Council in the Umbumbulu district.

90. First named Amanzimtoti Training Institute, Adams College was founded in 1853 by the American Board of Commissioners for Foreign Missions for the education of Africans. Renamed after Dr. Newton Adams, a medical missionary who died at Amanzimtoti mission station in 1847, the school was patterned after other elite African educational institutions.

91. Born in Boston, Massachusetts, Father John Ochs (1905-1957) joined the Oblates of Mary Immaculate in 1928 and was ordained in 1935 after completing his theological studies at the Catholic University in Washington, D.C. He moved to Natal in 1935 and served in Newcastle, Greyville, Dundee, and St. Paul's Parish in Durban. In 1953 he accepted an appointment as secretary for the Department of African Affairs of the Secretariate of the Southern African Catholic Bishop's Conference.

92. McCord Zulu Hospital was opened on Berea Hill, Durban in 1909. Its founder, Dr. James McCord, an American medical missionary, has written an account of his experiences, *My Patients Were Zulus* (New York: Rinehart, 1946).

93. Bennet Makalo Khaketla (1913-   ) was Lembede's roommate in Heilbron in the Orange Free State in the early 1940s. Born in the Qacha's Nek district, he moved to Lesotho in 1946 to take up a teaching post at Basutoland High School. With Ntsu Mokhehle, he edited *Mohlabani* (The Warrior), which vociferously attacked British colonial rule and served as a mouthpiece for the Basutoland African Congress. He was elected to the Legislative Council in 1960. After breaking with Mokhehle in late 1960, he joined the pro-monarchy Marema-Tlou Freedom Party. He was a journalist and a translator for the Bible Society. After the military coup ousting Leabua Jonathan in 1986, he was appointed Minister of Justice, a position he held until 1990. His book, *Lesotho 1970* (Berkeley: University of California Press, 1971) remains a standard work on the politics of that period. He is also a well-known dramatist (*Moshoeshoe le Baruti* (Morija: Sesuto Book Depot, 1947)), novelist (*Mosali a Nkhola* (Johannesburg: Afrikaanse Pers Boekhandel, 1960)), and poet (*Lipshamathe* (Pretoria: Afrikaanse Pers Bpk., 1954)).

94. Nicholas Lembede (1916-1976) was a student at Inkanyezi Primary School in Umbumbulu before attending Adams College and Mariannhill, where he completed his teachers' (T4) diploma. He maintained his home at the Lembede's homestead at Mphephetho, but taught at schools around Natal. He married his wife Phillipine in 1939.

95. Born near Alice, Julius Malie (1918-1970) moved to Pretoria as a youth

and grew up in his grandmother's home. Educated at Lovedale and the University of the Witwatersrand, he succeeded J. R. Rathebe as secretary of the Bantu Men's Social Centre. He also worked for the YMCA, the South African Institute of Race Relations, and the *Bantu World*. In the 1940s, he was active in the Left Club and the ANC Youth League, but in the 1950s he joined the Liberal Party. He took part in the Consultative Conference of African Leaders in December 1960 and was appointed to its continuation committee. He was arrested for his participation in the continuation committee and accused of furthering the aims of the ANC. He was convicted under the Suppression of Communism Act, but the charges were dropped on appeal. He left South Africa for Lesotho in mid-1961 and worked thereafter as a freelance journalist.

96. Born in Edinburgh in 1871, Prof. Thomas Miller Forsyth taught philosophy at Grey University College, Bloemfontein (1911–33) and Rhodes University (1941–44). He published *English Philosophy: A Study of Its Method and General Development* (London: A. and C. Black, 1910).

97. Cyril Edwin Mitchinson Joad is not usually listed in such august company. A British philosopher and professor at the University of London, he cultivated a broad audience in Britain after the First World War through his essays and radio broadcasts. He was part of the neorealist movement, which included such eminent figures as Alfred North Whitehead and Bertrand Russell. Among Joad's several dozen books are *Common-Sense Ethics* (London: Methuen and Co., 1921), *The Present and Future of Religion* (London: E. Benn, 1930), and *Guide to Philosophy* (London: V. Gollancz, 1936).

98. Born in Canada, Father Gerard Martin (1896–1977) entered the Oblates of Mary Immaculate (OMI) in 1917 and was ordained a priest in 1922. He was one of the first Canadian OMI priests assigned to Basutoland in 1923 and was a key figure in starting up a seminary for Basotho priests. From 1930 to 1933 he served as Administrator Apostolic until Bishop Bonhomme's arrival. He helped establish the Catholic printing works at Mazenod. He later moved to the Witwatersrand, where he was the Liaison Missionary Priest between families in Lesotho and family members working on mines. He also worked on missions in the West Rand and Soweto, including Orlando Township.

99. This Arabic quotation was cited by Arthur Barlow in a note following Walter Nhlapo's tribute to Lembede (*Barlow's Weekly*, 16 August 1947, p. 19).

100. A teacher, Victor Lembede (1929–1991) was principal of KwaSikhama Secondary School and owned several stores. He was killed at one of his stores in 1991, a victim of the internecine fighting in the Umbumbulu area.

101. Henry Wadsworth Longfellow, "A Psalm of Life."

102. James "Sofasonke" Mpanza (1889–1970) was a leading figure in squat-

ter movement politics in Orlando township. After serving a jail term for murder from 1914 to 1927, he became a teacher in Pretoria before moving to Johannesburg. In 1944, he responded to massive housing shortages by leading a movement of squatters outside Orlando. His Sofasonke Party was also active in township politics, and he was repeatedly elected to the Orlando Advisory Board.

103. A leading activist in Brakpan and the ANC Youth League, Joseph Malepe was voted on to the executive of the African National Congress. He also participated in the Transvaal African Teachers' Association (TATA), serving as its president from 1945 to 1947. In the 1950s, he joined Selope Thema's National-minded Bloc.

104. Born in Pimville, Paul Mosaka (1907–1963) studied at Healdtown and Fort Hare, where he completed a B.A. majoring in psychology and ethics. He taught at Healdtown before taking up a post at Moroka High School, Thaba 'Nchu. After moving to Orlando to run a general dealers' business owned by Dr. James Moroka, he became involved in politics. He was elected to the Natives Representative Council and was a founder of the African Democratic Party.

105. On 7 September 1946, Oriel Letuma Monongoaha led about 800 families to set up a shanty settlement at Pimville. His organization was the Pimville Sub-Tenants Vigilance Committee. The numbers soon swelled to 2,400 families. When the police ejected them, many of them moved to Orlando, where Monongoaha led most of them. They called themselves the "Homeless Ex-servicemen." Lembede provided legal advice for Monongoaha's group.

106. Yusuf Dadoo (1909–1983) was a Communist Party activist and a leading figure in the South African Indian Congress. He earned a medical degree at Edinburgh University. In 1945 he was elected president of the Transvaal Indian Congress; in 1950 he was chosen president of the South African Indian Congress. He was a leader of the anti-pass campaign in 1946. He promoted closer unity between the South African Indian Congress and the African National Congress. In 1952 he was jailed for his participation in the Defiance Campaign. In 1960 he left South Africa for Britain, where he remained prominent in anti-apartheid work. He joined the Communist Party in 1939. In 1972 he was elected chairman of the South African Communist Party, a position he retained until his death.

107. Ngubane went on to describe the interest in establishing a Lembede scholarship fund.

108. The ideas of Marcus Garvey, a Jamaican-born black nationalist, exploded on the South African scene after the First World War. Founder of the Universal Negro Improvement Association in Jamaica in 1914, he trans-

planted his movement to New York in 1916 and developed a large following in the United States and throughout the black world. His organization had a strong presence in Cape Town and had chapters scattered throughout the rest of South Africa. Garvey's promotion of black self-reliance, positive self-images and black unity had a profound influence on black South Africans on many levels. The apex of Garvey's influence was in the 1920s, but his ideas were debated in African political circles in South Africa for several more decades. The Garvey movement in South Africa is given extensive treatment in Robert Hill and Greg Pirio, "'Africa for the Africans': The Garvey Movement in South Africa, 1920–1940," in *The Politics of Race, Class & Nationalism in Twentieth Century South Africa,* edited by Shula Marks and Stanley Trapido, 209–53. London: Longman, 1987.

Bibliography

Abraham, Peter. *Tell Freedom: Memories of Africa*. London: Faber and Faber, 1954.

Basner, Miriam. *Am I an African? The Political Memoirs of H. M. Basner*. Johannesburg: Witwatersrand University Press, 1993.

Bonner, Philip. "The Politics of Black Squatter Movements on the Rand, 1944-1952." *Radical History Review* 46/7 (1990): 89-116.

Bradford, Helen. *A Taste of Freedom: The ICU in Rural South Africa, 1924-1930*. New Haven: Yale University Press, 1987.

Brookes, Edgar. *A South African Pilgrimage*. Johannesburg: Ravan Press, 1977.

Bruce, Dickson. "Ancient Africa and the Early Black American Historians, 1883-1915." *American Quarterly* XXXVI (1984): 684-699.

Bundy, Colin. "The Abolition of the Masters and Servants Act," *South African Labour Bulletin* 2 (May-June 1975): 37-46.

Callinicos, Luli. *A Place in the City: The Rand on the Eve of Apartheid*. Johannesburg: Ravan Press, 1993.

Carter, Gwendolen and Thomas Karis. *From Protest to Challenge: A Documentary History of African Politics in South Africa, 1882-1964*. Vol. II. Stanford: Hoover Institution Press, 1973.

Charney, Craig. "Pixley Seme '06: Father of the African National Congress." *Columbia College Today* 14 (2) (Spring/Summer 1987): 15-17.

Cosgrove, Richard. *The Rule of Law: Albert Venn Dicey: Victorian Jurist*. Chapel Hill: University of North Carolina Press, 1980.

Couzens, Tim. *The New African: A Study of the Life and Work of H. I. E. Dhlomo*. Johannesburg: Ravan Press, 1985.

Davenport, T. R. "African Townsmen? South African Natives (Urban Areas) Legislation Through the Years." *African Affairs* 68 (271) (1969): 95-109.

Davies, Robert. "The Class Character of South Africa's Industrial Conciliation Legislation." *South African Labour Bulletin* 2 (6) (1976).

Davis, Dennis with Robert Fine. *Beyond Apartheid: Labour and Liberation in South Africa*. Johannesburg: Ravan Press, 1991.

Davis, R. Hunt. "The Black American Educational Component in African

Responses to Colonialism in South Africa." *Journal of Southern African Affairs* 3 (1) (1968): 69–84.

———. "John L. Dube: A South African Exponent of Booker T. Washington." *Journal of African Studies* 2 (1975–76): 497–528.

Dubow, Saul. *Racial Segregation and the Origins of Apartheid in South Africa, 1919–1936.* New York: St. Martin's Press, 1989.

Forman, Sadie and Andre Odendaal. *A Trumpet From the Housetops: The Selected Writings of Lionel Forman.* Cape Town: David Philip, 1992.

Forsyth, Thomas Miller. *English Philosophy: A Study of its Method and General Development.* London: A. and C. Black, 1910.

Furlong, Patrick. *Between Crown and Swastika: The Impact of the Radical Right on the Afrikaner Nationalist Movement in the Fascist Era.* Middletown, Ct.: Wesleyan University Press, 1991.

Gangulee, N., ed. *Giuseppe Mazzini: Selected Writings.* Westport, Ct.: Greenwood Press, 1974.

Gerard, Albert. *Four African Literatures: Xhosa, Sotho, Zulu, Amharic.* Berkeley: University of California Press, 1971.

Gerhart, Gail. *Black Power in South Africa.* Berkeley: University of California Press, 1978.

Harlan, Louis. "Booker T. Washington and the White Man's Burden." *American Historical Review* 71 (2) (1966): 441–67.

———. *Booker T. Washington: The Making of a Black Leader, 1856–1901.* New York: Oxford University Press, 1972.

Hill, Robert and Greg Pirio. "'Africa for the Africans': The Garvey Movement in South Africa, 1920–1940," In *The Politics of Race, Class and Nationalism in Twentieth-Century South Africa,* edited by Shula Marks and Stanley Trapido, 209–53. London: Longman, 1987.

Hirson, Baruch. *Yours for the Union: Class and Community Struggles in South Africa.* Johannesburg: Witwatersrand University Press, 1989.

Holm, John and Patrick Molutsi, eds. *Democracy in Botswana.* Gaborone, Botswana: Macmillan Botswana Publishing Company, 1989.

Kunene, Dan. *Thomas Mofolo and the Emergence of Written Sesotho Prose.* Johannesburg: Ravan Press, 1989.

Kuper, Adam. *Wives for Cattle: Bridewealth and Marriage in Southern Africa.* London: Routledge and Kegan Paul, 1982.

Kurth, Peter. *American Cassandra: The Life of Dorothy Thompson.* Boston: Little, Brown and Co., 1990.

Lodge, Tom. *Black Politics in South Africa Since 1945.* London: Longman, 1983.

Lynch, Hollis. *Edward Wilmot Blyden Pan-Negro Patriot 1832–1912.* London: Oxford University Press, 1967.

Mackenzie, Alexander. *Propaganda Boom.* London: J. Gifford, 1938.

McCord, James. *My Patients Were Zulus.* New York: Rinehart, 1946.

Marable, Manning. "Booker T. Washington and African Nationalism." *Phylon* 35 (1974): 398–406.

Marks, Shula. *Reluctant Rebellion: The 1906-8 Disturbances in Natal.* Oxford: Clarendon Press, 1970.

Maylam, Paul. "The Rise and Decline of Urban Apartheid in South Africa," *African Affairs* 89 (354) (1990): 57–84.

Mda, A. P. (pseudonym umAfrika). "Anton Lembede — III." *The Africanist* (July/August 1955): 2–4.

Packard, Randall. *White Plague, Black Labour: Tuberculosis and the Political Economy of Health and Disease in South Africa.* Berkeley: University of California Press, 1989.

Peires, Jeffrey. "The Lovedale Press: Literature for the Bantu Revisited." *History in Africa* 6 (1979): 155–175.

Peteni, Randall. *Hill of Fools: A Novel of the Ciskei.* London: Heinemann, 1976.

————. *Towards Tomorrow: The Story of the African Teacher's Associations of South Africa.* Algonac, Michigan: Reference Publications, 1979.

Plaatje, Solomon. *Native Life in South Africa.* London: P. S. King and Son, 1916.

Rive, Richard and Tim Couzens. *Seme: The Founder of the ANC.* Johannesburg: Skotaville Publishers, 1991.

Sanders, Marion. *Dorothy Thompson: A Legend in Her Times.* Boston: Houghton Mifflin, 1973.

Saunders, A. J. G. M. "Anton Muziwakhe Lembede — Pioneer of African Nationalism." *Codicillus* XXVII (2) (1981): 11–17.

Saunders, Christopher. "Pixley Seme: Towards a Biography." *South African Historical Journal* 25 (1991): 196–217.

Schimlek, Francis. *Mariannhill: A Study in Bantu Life and Missionary Effort.* Mariannhill: Mariannhill Mission Press, 1953.

————. *Mariannhill and its Apostolate.* Reimlingen via Nordlingen, Germany: St. Joseph Mission Press, 1964.

Smith Edwin. *Aggrey of Africa: A Study in Black and White.* London: Student Christian Movement Press, 1929.

Tatz, C. M. *Shadow and Substance in South Africa: A Study in Land and Franchise Politics Affecting Africans, 1910-1960.* Pietermaritzburg: University of Natal Press, 1962.

Walshe, Peter. *The Rise of African Nationalism in South Africa: The African National Congress, 1912-1957.* Berkeley: University of California Press, 1971.

Willan, Brian. *Sol Plaatje: A Biography*. Berkeley: University of California Press, 1984.

Wylie, Diana. *A Little God: The Twilight of Patriarchy in a Southern African Chiefdom*. Hanover: University Press of New England, 1990.

Index

About the Editors

Luyanda ka Msumza was born and raised in Ginsberg Location in King William's Town in the eastern Cape. He went into exile from South Africa in 1978 and was employed as a coordinator at the Transformation Resource Center in Maseru, Lesotho. In 1990 he returned to South Africa and worked at the Quaker Peace Center in Cape Town as a manager for the Center's Peace Process Program and its Community Mediation Service. In 1996 he was appointed provincial coordinator for the Eastern Cape for the South African government's Special Fund for Political Prisoners, Returned Exiles, Banned Persons, and Widows of Political Prisoners. At various times he has studied at the Oxford Air Training School in Great Britain, New Hampshire College in the United States, and the University of Cape Town.

Robert Edgar is a Professor in the Department of African Studies at Howard University in Washington, D.C. He has also taught at the National University of Lesotho, Georgetown University and the University of Virginia. He is the author of *Prophets With Honour: A Documentary History of Lekhotla la Bafo* (1986); *Because They Chose the Plan of God: The Story of the Bulhoek Massacre* (1987); *Sanctioning Apartheid* (1990); and *An African American in South Africa: The Travel Notes of Ralph J. Bunche, 1937* (1992). In 1994-1995 he was the recipient of a Fulbright Fellowship for research in South Africa and Lesotho.

WHEN a group of young political activists met in 1944 to launch the African National Congress Youth League, it included the nucleus of a remarkable generation of leaders who forged the struggle for freedom and equality in South Africa for the next half century: Nelson Mandela, Oliver Tambo, Walter Sisulu, Jordan Ngubane, Ellen Kuzwayo, Albertina Smith, A. P. Mda, Dan Tloome, and David Bopape. It was Anton Lembede, however, whom they chose as their first president.

Lembede, who had just begun practicing law in Johannesburg, was known for his sharp intellect, fiery personality, and unwavering commitment to the struggle at hand. The son of farm laborers from the district of Georgedale, Natal, Lembede had worked tirelessly to put himself through school and college, and then to qualify for the bachelor of laws degree. When he began law practice in 1943, he had also earned the respect of his fellows, not only for his intellectual achievements (which were many), but also for his dedication to the cause of freedom in South Africa. "I am," he explained, "Africa's own child."

His untimely death in 1947 at the age of 33 sent a wave of grief through the Congress Youth, who had looked to him for moral as well as political leadership. With the publication of FREEDOM iN OUR LIFETIME, the editors acknowledge Lembede's early contribution to the freedom movement, in particular his passionate and eloquent articulation of the African-centered philosophy he called "Africanism."